STUDIES IN PHILOSOPHY

V

JOHN DEWEY'S THEORY
OF
INQUIRY AND TRUTH

by

LOWELL NISSEN

University of Arkansas

1966

MOUTON & CO.

THE HAGUE · PARIS

Printed in The Netherlands.

To My Parents

PREFACE

John Dewey's avowed intention in developing his account of inquiry was to make the methodology of science available to other disciplines, with particular interest in terminating the endless controversy in philosophy and in making it possible for the progress common in science, particularly physical science, to be shared by the studies of how man might better live. By applying the methodology of science he hoped to achieve both an intellectual victory, and a cultural and humanistic one.

This study, however, is not concerned with evaluating the application of Dewey's account of inquiry, but with evaluating the account, itself.

Since this account finds its most recent and complete expression in his *Logic: The Theory of Inquiry*, it is from this volume that most of the passages are taken. Furthermore, since in Dewey's scheme of things, truth is tied intimately to inquiry (for Dewey made truth an offspring of inquiry) the study of his account of inquiry is followed by a shorter appraisal of his account of truth.

Much, if not indeed most, philosophical criticism involves a statement by the critic of the view he is criticizing. The danger in such a procedure is that he may misstate that view. It seemed to me, therefore, that it would be better to work directly from quoted passages.

Misunderstanding may still occur (although I try to minimize this possibility by offering alternative interpretations), but the error will not, at least, be that of misleading the reader on what Dewey said, and whatever error of interpretation remains will stand exposed where the reader may detect it.

Preface

I wish to thank Professor Robert Dewey for his counsel and helpful criticism and my wife Beverly without whose help the whole study would like this very awkward read.

LOWELL NISSEN

CONTENTS

I

THE ANTECEDENT CONDITIONS OF INQUIRY

Inquiry is described by John Dewey as a transformation of an indeterminate situation into a determinate one. The indeterminate situation constitutes the antecedent conditions of inquiry. This chapter will be devoted to examining Dewey's concepts of a situation and an indeterminate situation.

In order to introduce the concepts of the situation and the indeterminate situation and, indeed, the whole subject of inquiry, let us look first at a definition of "inquiry". Dewey writes, *"Inquiry is the controlled or directed transformation of an indeterminate situation into one that is so determinate in its constituent distinctions and relations as to convert the elements of the original situation into a unified whole."* [1]

One's first impression is that this definition is too narrow and that it is a definition of what might be called "successful inquiry", that is, inquiry plus the answer. Ordinarily the verb, "to inquire", is used as an approximate synonym for such verbs as, "to question", "to seek", "to look for", "to investigate", "to examine", "to search", and the like. The word, "question", and the word, "answer", are used in such a way that, although an answer implies that there has been a question, a question does not imply that there will be an answer. We might imagine a traveler asking a deaf resident the directions to the theater. That the man does not answer does not mean that the traveler did not ask. Dewey's definition of "inquiry", defining, as it does, only "successful inquiry", would make it hard to give meaning to such a sen-

---

[1] John Dewey, *Logic: The Theory of Inquiry* (New York, 1938), pp. 104-105.

tence as, "The inquiry was unsuccessful." "Inquiry" is defined in such a way that, if it were unsuccessful, it would not be called "inquiry".

It is not, of course, necessary that one always follow accepted meanings. However, it should be clear when one does not so that communication is possible. In the case of the definition of "inquiry" Dewey does not appear to be aware that he has altered the meaning of the word. Furthermore, since Dewey is concerned in his *Logic: The Theory of Inquiry* to set forth the methods of successful as over against unsuccessful inquiry, he does not consistently keep to his own definition.

A second defect of the definition is that it is too broad. It reads in part, "*Inquiry is the controlled or directed transformation of an indeterminate situation into one that is so determinate in its constituent distinctions and relations . . .*" [2] As Bertrand Russell has noted, the building of a brick wall from a pile of bricks and the changes which take place when a disorganized squad of men is taken over by a drill sergeant both fit Dewey's definition of "inquiry".[3] The pile of bricks, the soldiers standing about are, relative to how things are later, indeterminate. In each case there is change from disorder to order, and in each case the change is directed. Furthermore, the brick wall and the soldiers, dressed right and covered down, may each be described as "a unified whole". There is no reason why, under the terms of the definition, the building of a wall and a parade ground exercise should not be considered inquiry. To Russell's two examples could be added many others. According to Dewey's definition a beaver building a dam is engaged in inquiry. So is a cook preparing a meal or a gardener weeding the flowers. Indeed, few human activities are not directed and do not bring about some sort of new order. Even inanimate machines could be said to be engaged in inquiry; for example, a bookbinding machine takes the pages, the cardboard, the cloth, the glue, and the thread and combines them into a unified whole.

---

[2] Dewey, *Logic*, pp. 104-105.
[3] Bertrand Russell, *A History of Western Philosophy* (New York, 1945), p. 823.

Dewey does not, of course, intend to call any of these examples "inquiry". The definition, therefore, is too broad. It includes much, very much, that no one, including Dewey, would consider as inquiry.

A. THE SITUATION

Soldiers milling about and a pile of bricks were offered as illustrating indeterminate situations. Actually, of course, one cannot be sure that these examples are suitable until one understands what Dewey means by "indeterminate situation". However, understanding what he means by "indeterminate situation" requires first understanding what he means by "situation". To help the reader Dewey indicates in a footnote directly following the definition of "inquiry" that the word, "situation", is to be understood as explained on pages sixty-six and sixty-seven of the *Logic*. Here he writes, "I begin the discussion by introducing and explaining the denotative force of the word *situation*. Its import may perhaps be most readily indicated by means of a preliminary negative statement. What is designated by the word 'situation' is *not* a single object or event or set of objects and events." One wonders if Dewey means that objects and events may be a part of a situation but that a situation is merely more than these; or if he means that they are not even parts of a situation. If the former, what more is there? If the latter, what does consitute a situation? Furthermore, it would help to understand the significance of saying that a situation is not an object or event if one knew what he means by "object" and "event".

Dewey proceeds to give a reason for saying that a situation is not a single object or event or sets of them: "For we never experience nor form judgments about objects and events in isolation, but only in connection with a contextual whole." [4] This passage is easily misunderstood. Dewey does not mean that we never experience a single object or event or form judgments of either, for such a statement could easily be refuted. When one bumps into a

---

[4] Dewey, *Logic*, p. 66.

chair while groping in the dark to get a glass of water, he certainly experiences a single object, and when one watches a race during track season, he certainly experiences a single event. What Dewey means is that in experiencing a single object, one experiences more than that object. When one collides with a chair, part of the total experience is that it is dark, that one is sleepy and thirsty, etc.

Similarly, when Dewey says that one never forms judgments about an object in isolation, he does not mean to deny that one may judge, for example, that his desk is brown or that his chair is decidedly uncomfortable. What he denies is simply the notion that there is no context surrounding the judgment. He is insisting, and rightly so, that all judgments are made within a context.

We have read what a situation is not. Here is a statement in which Dewey says what a situation is. For clarity, the preceding sentence is repeated. "For we never experience nor form judgments about objects and events in isolation, but only in connection with a contextual whole. This latter is what is called a 'situation'." [5] A contextual whole is called a "situation". Dewey apparently means this not as a case of class inclusion, but as a statement of equivalence so that a contextual whole is a situation and a situation is a contextual whole.

Perhaps the major objection to defining "situation" as a context is that this makes it absurd to have inquiry acting on the situation. Inquiry concerns, indeed, especially concerns, that which is the center of attention, and it more or less ignores the rest. Yet it is precisely what is in practice ignored that Dewey makes the material for inquiry when he says that the situation is a context. Defining "situation" as a context is incompatible with the role a situation must play in inquiry.

The above passage from Dewey carries with it the suggestion that the nature of a situation is tied up with what experiences and judgments are, for he began, "For we never experience nor form judgments about objects and events in isolation . . ." The similarity with judgments is not developed, but the similarity with experience is. "In actual experience, there is never any such isolated

[5]   Dewey, *Logic*, p. 66.

singular object or event; *an* object or event is always a special part, phase, or aspect, of an environing experienced world – a situation." [6] This passage surely suggests that the limits of a situation are set by experience, indeed, that the limits of an experience are the limits of a situation. Dewey, in fact, elsewhere writes, "Other criticisms of my theory of experience are connected with the fact that I have called experiences *situations* . . ." [7]

Since it seems reasonably certain that by "situation" Dewey means experience, it would seem that the way to understand what Dewey means by "situation" is to find out what he means by "experience". "Things interacting in certain ways *are* experience . . ." [8]

"According to the naturalistic view, every experience in its direct occurrence is an interaction of environing conditions and an organism." [9] The things interacting are an organism and the world. If experience *is* interaction between an organism and the world (and not merely a *result* of such interaction), is the person included in each experience? Dewey seems to imply this when he says, "Things interacting in certain ways *are* experience; they are what is experienced." [10] He says it somewhat more directly another place, where, in criticizing another approach, he writes, ". . . this ignoring leaves on our hands the 'me', or knowing self, as a separate thing within which experience falls (instead of its falling in a specifiable place within experience) . . ." [11] Surely the only way one can sensibly say that he experiences himself as a part of each of his experiences is to include within the concept of experience far more than the objects of awareness. This is precisely what Dewey (at least on occasion) does.

---

[6]   Dewey, *Logic*, p. 67.
[7]   *The Philosophy of John Dewey*, ed. Paul Arthur Schilpp (New York, 1951), p. 544.
[8]   John Dewey, *Experience and Nature*, Dover edition (New York, 1958), p. 4a.
[9]   *The Philosophy of John Dewey*, p. 544.
[10]   Dewey, *Experience and Nature*, p. 4a.
[11]   John Dewey, *Essays in Experimental Logic*, Dover edition (New York), p. 71.

"Consciousness", in other words, is only a very small and shifting portion of experience.[12]

"Experience" denotes the planted field, the sowed seeds, the reaped harvests, the changes of night and day, spring and autumn, wet and dry, heat and cold, that are observed, feared, longed for; it also denotes the one who plants and reaps, who works and rejoices, hopes, fears, plans, invokes magic or chemistry to aid him, who is downcast or triumphant. It is "double-barrelled" in that it recognizes in its primary integrity no division between act and material, subject and object, but contains them both in an unanalyzed totality.[13]

If experience includes the organism and all that it interacts with, where does Dewey set the limits? Things could get out of hand and lead to the position that every experience is of the whole universe and of all time. Suppose that one is typing.

The word which I have just written is momentarily focal; around it there shade off into vagueness my typewriter, the desk, the room, the building, the campus, the town, and so on. *In* the experience, and in it in such a way as to *qualify* even what is shiningly apparent, are all the physical features of the environment extending out into space no one can say how far, and all the habits and interests extending backward and forward in time, of the organism which uses the typewriter and which notes the written form of the word only as temporary focus in a vast and changing scene . . . I shall only point out that when the word "experience" is employed in the text it means just such an immense and operative world of diverse and interacting elements.[14]

In saying ". . . no one can say how far . . ." Dewey seems to be saying that boundaries of an experience cannot be drawn. This is a rather serious matter because experience is a fundamental concept for Dewey and one that is necessary in understanding the initial stage of inquiry. If the boundaries of an experience cannot be drawn, neither can those of a situation. Russell feels that Dewey is committed to the view that a situation includes the whole universe. ". . . I do not see how, on Dr. Dewey's principles, a 'situation' can embrace less than the whole universe; this is an inevitable consequence of the insistence upon continuity." [15]

---

[12] Dewey, *Essays*, p. 6.
[13] Dewey, *Experience and Nature*, p. 8.
[14] Dewey, *Essays*, pp. 6-7.
[15] *The Philosophy of John Dewey*, p. 139.

Dewey denies this, of course, but his denial has the effect only of affirming that he personally does not hold a universe-view of a situation.[16] His denial does not show that he is not logically committed to that view. It may be hasty to conclude with Russell that Dewey is, indeed, committed to that view, but it must be acknowledged that the gate is ajar when Dewey says that experience (and, therefore, a situation) includes much more than the range of consciousness.

One might feel, however, that Dewey draws the necessary boundaries when he says,

The living creature undergoes, suffers, the consequences of its own behavior. This close connection between doing and suffering or undergoing forms what we call experience. Disconnected doing and disconnected suffering are neither of them experiences. Suppose fire encroaches upon a man when he is asleep. Part of his body is burned away. The burn does not perceptibly result from what he has done. There is nothing which in any instructive way can be named experience. Or again there is a series of mere activities, like twitchings of muscles in a spasm. The movements amount to nothing; they have no consequences for life. Or, if they have, these consequences are not connected with prior doing. There is no experience, no learning, no cumulative process. But suppose a busy infant puts his finger in the fire; the doing is random, aimless, without intention or reflection. But something happens in consequence. The child undergoes heat, he suffers pain. The doing and undergoing, the reaching and the burn, are connected. One comes to suggest and mean the other. Then there is experience in a vital and significant sense.[17]

Although one might feel that there is not a sufficient difference between the examples of the burned man and the burned child (the man's sleeping where and when he did can be regarded as just as genuine an action as the child's extending a finger into the fire, and as suitable for being the occasion for learning), clearly Dewey is saying that the interaction of organism and environment is not experience unless learning takes place. It is equally clear that this new qualification of the nature of an experience sets boundaries to the concept of experience. Were Russell reviewing

[16] *The Philosophy of John Dewey*, pp. 544-545.
[17] John Dewey, *Reconstruction in Philosophy*, Beacon edition (Boston, 1957), pp. 86-87.

Dewey's *Reconstruction in Philosophy* instead of his *Logic*, he could not accuse Dewey of inadvertent holism. The passage removes from Dewey's side the thorn of the rose in the crannied wall, but replaces it with the sharper barb of inconsistency. Unless Dewey subscribes to the thesis that most of our learning is unconscious (and the passage above speaks to the contrary), the fact that he limits experience to occasions of learning is not compatible with his saying elsewhere that consciousness covers only a small part of experience.

Returning to Dewey's discussion of the meaning of "situation", we read,

In actual experience, there is never any such isolated singular object or event; *an* object or event is always a special part, phase, or aspect, of an environing experienced world – a situation. The singular object stands out conspicuously because of its especially focal and crucial position at a given time in determination of some problem of use or enjoyment which the *total* complex environment presents. There is always a *field* in which observation of *this* or *that* object or event occurs.[18]

One is reminded of Gestalt psychology. There is this difference, however: the Gestaltists contrast the figure per se with the field, but Dewey does not contrast objects and events *per se* with the situation. He contrasts only a particular object or event. Such a choice of words would allow the field to include other objects and events. The field would then be contrasted with this or that object or event not because it, the field, contained no objects or events, but because its objects and events were not the center of attention. What is the field and what is not would then be determined not by what is out there, but by the focus of attention of the person engaged in the interaction. Thus we have something very much like the statement that a situation is a context, and it is, of course, open to the same objection.

Perhaps by "field" Dewey means something like a field of force as used in physics in reference to, say, magnetic attraction or gravity. "Other criticisms of my theory of experience are connected with the fact that I have called experiences *situations*,

18   Dewey, *Logic*, p. 67.

my use of the word antedating, I suppose, the introduction of the *field* idea in physical theory, but nevertheless employed, as far as I can see, to meet pretty much the same need . . ." [19] He then explains that this need is to find an alternative to an atomism which denies all connections and a block monism which denies plurality and the discrete. Although it is clear that Dewey wants to tread a middle ground, it is not at all clear that borrowing the concept of a physical field is particularly helpful. The Gestalt field seems more relevant.

Dewey now adds a quite different point regarding the nature of a situation. "Recurring to the main topic, it is to be remarked that a situation is a whole in virtue of its immediately pervasive quality. When we describe it from the psychological side, we have to say that the situation as a qualitative whole is sensed or *felt*." [20] In the text from which this is taken Dewey then compares this quality which a situation is said to have, not with such qualities as red, hard, or sweet, but with such qualities as distressing, perplexing, cheerful, and disconsolate. Indeed, this quality, which is the identifying mark of a situation, is surprisingly like the qualities of the indeterminate situation at the beginning of inquiry and the unified situation at the end. Dewey also compares the quality which distinguishes something as a situation to the tertiary qualities of Santyana and to the pervading quality of a picture which marks it as a Rembrandt or a Titian. Nevertheless, it is also different, for this quality, which Dewey finds in every situation, is such that no two situations are ever alike. "The pervasively qualitative is not only that which binds all constituents into a whole but it is also unique; it constitutes in each situation an *individual* situation, indivisible and unduplicable." [21] Each situation is unique, and the reason for its being unique is that it has a unique quality.

It seems, however, to be highly unlikely that there could be any one quality which has so many discernible gradations as to be different for each situation. Furthermore, when Dewey says that

[19] *The Philosophy of John Dewey*, p. 544.
[20] Dewey, *Logic*, p. 68.
[21] Dewey, *Logic*, p. 68.

this pervading quality is what constitutes each situation as an individual situation, he apparently excludes anything else from performing that function. The fact of the matter is, however, that experiences differ from one another in countless ways other than by some pervading quality. For example, on a certain occasion one sees the sun shining, while on another he sees an overcast sky. Any situation experienced in which a person sees the sun shining will be different from one in which he sees an overcast sky. Yet neither the experience of seeing the sun nor of seeing an overcast sky has any right to be called a pervading quality of the situation, much less one which cannot be repeated.

Although the concept of a situation is fundamental to Dewey's account of inquiry, it has been shown that the explanation of that concept is marred by serious faults. On the positive side, however, it seems reasonable to say that Dewey means to associate "situation" very closely (and perhaps identify it) with both "context" and "experience", and that "experience" is to be very broadly conceived.

B.   THE INDETERMINATE SITUATION

Contrary to what one might suppose, Dewey's indeterminate situation is not completely indeterminate, for he writes, "The first step in answering this question is to recognize that no situation which is *completely* indeterminate can possibly be converted into a problem having definite constituents." [22] Dewey goes on to give the example of a fire in an assembly hall. Certain features are determinate, for example, the location of aisles, of exits, and of the fire. The indeterminate situation is, therefore, only partially indeterminate.

Another item which should be considered for explanatory purposes is that the indeterminate situation is not regarded by Dewey as the result of something the inquirer does. It is something he finds himself in, not something he creates. "The indeterminate situation comes into existence from existential causes, just as does,

[22]   Dewey, *Logic*, p. 108.

say, the organic imbalance of hunger." [23] By saying that the indeterminate situation comes into existence from existential causes Dewey means only that the person does not have a hand in it. One sometimes finds himself in an indeterminate situation just as one sometimes finds himself hungry; and, as a matter of fact, finding oneself hungry is an example of finding oneself in an indeterminate situation.

A closely related characteristic attributed to this stage of inquiry is that it is not something cognitive. "There is nothing intellectual or cognitive in the existence of such situations, although they are the necessary condition of cognitive operations or inquiry. In themselves they are precognitive." [24] Presumably this is another way of saying that an indeterminate situation is something that happens to one, and not something the mind constructs. This fits well with the overall view that the initial situation is objectively, rather than subjectively, indeterminate.

However, it may be that Dewey considers a situation cognitive only if it is the product of inquiry. Then to say that the indeterminate situation is precognitive is to say only that it comes before inquiry.

With these passages out of the way let us now turn to those which are more directly concerned with explaining what Dewey means by "indeterminate situation".

The original indeterminate situation is not only "open" to inquiry, but it is open in the sense that its constituents do not hang together ... Thus it is of the very nature of the indeterminate situation which evokes inquiry to be *questionable*; or, in terms of actuality instead of potentiality, to be uncertain, unsettled, disturbed ... A variety of names serves to characterize indeterminate situations. They are disturbed, troubled, ambiguous, confused, full of conflicting tendencies, obscure, etc.[25]

Let us try to fit these passages to an example. Since Dewey's theory of inquiry is meant to cover all inquiry, any example should do. Let us suppose that a physician is examining a sick man. The physician, then, is engaged in inquiry. From the defini-

---

23   Dewey, *Logic*, p. 107.
24   Dewey, *Logic*, p. 107.
25   Dewey, *Logic*, p. 105.

tion of "inquiry" we understand that the first stage of inquiry is the indeterminate situation. This information can be used to help identify the indeterminate situation. To aid further in this identification, here is an excerpt from one of the passages already quoted: "Thus it is of the very nature of the indeterminate situation which evokes inquiry . . ." We should be able, therefore, to find the indeterminate situation by looking for that which evokes inquiry. In the example before us what is it which does this? Apparently, it is the sick man.

The sick man is said, then, to be indeterminate. However, it is rather difficult to understand how a sick man can be indeterminate. We might say that the doctor has not yet determined why the man is ill, so perhaps in an awkward sort of way we could say that, to the doctor, the sick man is indeterminate. A more straightforward way of phrasing this would be to say simply that the doctor does not know why the man is ill. However, Dewey adds, "It is the *situation* that has these traits. *We* are doubtful because the situation is inherently doubtful." [26] To make it even more clear, he also says, "It is, accordingly, a mistake to suppose that a situation is doubtful only in a 'subjective' sense." [27] Applied to the example before us, this means that Dewey insists that the indeterminacy qualifies the sick man, not the extent of the doctor's knowledge about him.

If one must find some meaning to saying that the sick man is indeterminate, perhaps one could say that the qualities of the man were somehow indistinct. There then seem to be two courses available. The first is to say that the man simply does not possess definite qualities. That is to say, although he has weight, he does not have a definite weight. Although he has warmth, he does not have a definite temperature. Although his blood has white corpuscles, he does not have a definite white blood count. This interpretation is, of course, absurd.

The other way in which one might try to make sense out of the statement that the qualities of the sick man are indeterminate is to say that although he possesses weight, it is not great enough to

[26] Dewey, *Logic*, pp. 105-106.
[27] Dewey, *Logic*, p. 106.

say definitely that he is overweight, neither low enough to be certain that he is not. Although he possesses a temperature above normal, it is not high enough to warrant considering him sick, nor low enough to be a reason for considering him well. Although his blood contains white corpuscles, the count is neither so high that he clearly has an infection, nor so low that one may conclude that he has not. Whatever virtue such an interpretation may have, and it seems to have none, it is obviously foreign to Dewey's intentions. Moreover, since the qualities of most things do not fall into such borderline areas, this view would mean that most situations at the start of inquiry were determinate, not indeterminate.

As we have already seen, Dewey offers other terms in place of the term, "indeterminate". These are "disturbed", "troubled", "ambiguous", "confused", "full of conflicting tendencies", "obscure", and "doubtful". Perhaps one might feel that these terms do fit some situations by themselves. If it is a person who is the subject of inquiry, the initial situation may indeed be disturbed, troubled, ambiguous, and so on. The sick man may be disturbed, for example, because the physician is late. He may be troubled because his pain persists. What he tells the doctor might be ambiguous. Surely he could be full of conflicting tendencies, for he might wish both to return to work and to take care of his health. Perhaps he could be said to be obscure, but this, too, would surely pertain to something he says. Of course, he may very well be doubtful about many things.

All of these are ways in which an initial situation could legitimately be described as disturbed, troubled, ambiguous, etc., and be said to have these characteristics independently of the inquirer. Is this what Dewey means? No, indeed. The disturbed and troubled character of the situation is a characteristic which successful inquiry removes. That is what Dewey means when he says that it is a characteristic of the *initial* situation. If, however, the disturbance of the sick man were due, as suggested in this example, to the fact that the doctor was late in coming, the patient may very well have remained disturbed even after the diagnosis was completed. Similarly, since a diagnosis does not remove pain, if he were troubled because of his pain, he would have remained troubled even after the diagnosis. So also with the other characteristics. Under this interpretation of the expression, "indeterminate situation", the disturbed and troubled character of the initial situation is not removed by successful inquiry. Since, according to Dewey's definition, the indeterminacy is removed by inquiry, this interpretation cannot be what Dewey means.

As soon as one takes an example in which the initial situation is something inanimate, the various properties Dewey ascribes to it do not even seem to be applicable. Suppose a geologist is examining a rock, trying to identify it. In doing so he is engaged in inquiry. Since the rock is that which evokes the examination, it apparently is what Dewey would call the "initial situation". The initial situation, Dewey says, is indeterminate. Presumably this would mean that the rock is indeterminate. It must also be said to be disturbed, troubled, ambiguous, obscure, full of conflicting tendencies, and doubtful. That there may be no misunderstanding about what it is that has these characteristics, Dewey adds that it is the situation which possesses these traits and that we are doubtful only because the situation is itself doubtful. Perhaps a rock can be obscure in a sense if it is hidden in the underbrush, and, of course, it can be disturbed simply by dislodging it. This, however, is hardly what Dewey means, for in his sense of "obscure" the rock may remain obscure even after the geologist is peering closely at it, since it remains obscure until the inquiry is concluded. It may aid the examination to dislodge the rock, but that fact is totally irrelevant to the sense of "disturb" that Dewey means when he implies that every rock which is the subject of inquiry is, at the initiation of that inquiry, disturbed. There seems to be no sense whatsoever to saying that a rock can be troubled, doubtful, or that it can be full of conflicting tendencies.

An examination of what Dewey means by "indeterminate situation" must give prominent place to what Dewey, himself, says about it. He writes, "The situation in which it occurs is indeterminate, therefore, with respect to its *issue*." [28] This passage taken out of context appears to be speaking in general terms about the

[28]   Dewey, *Logic*, p. 106.

situation. The reason for it, however, is to explain the use of "indeterminate" in respect to inquiry. In terms of inquiry it now seems that all Dewey means by calling the initial situation "indeterminate" is that the outcome is unknown. The "outcome of inquiry" or the "issue of inquiry", however, is subject to several quite different interpretations. First, does Dewey mean that the issue of the inquiry is unknown to everyone, even to those not conducting the inquiry; or does he mean only that it is unknown to the one engaged in the inquiry? Secondly, when he speaks of the issue of inquiry, does he mean the issue of a particular inquiry by a certain person at a certain time, or does he mean the issue of successful inquiry?

If he means that the issue of inquiry is unknown to everyone, then, whether he has in mind successful inquiry only or both successful and unsuccessful inquiry, he is mistaken. Consider an example in which Dewey would be wrong in regard to successful inquiry. An automobile mechanic would be not at all uncertain about the issue of successful inquiry conducted by someone else into how to start a car on a cold morning. Competence in a given field is to know the correct issue of numerous possible inquiries within that field. An example in which one knows the outcome of an unsuccessful inquiry might be the following: a mother sets for her child a task clearly beyond his ability, for example, to find out how the pieces of a difficult puzzle fit together. Since she knows her child well, she is able to predict that the inquiry will end by his growing impatient and throwing the pieces on the floor. This, let us suppose, is what happens. Therefore, we must say that the mother knew the issue of this unsuccessful inquiry.

It is, of course, unlikely that Dewey means that an indeterminate situation is one whose issue is unknown to everyone. It is more probable that he means that it is unknown to the person conducting the inquiry. Even with this much settled we must consider two further interpretations. By "issue" does Dewey mean the issue of an inquiry conducted by a particular person at a certain time, or does he mean the issue of successful inquiry?

The former kind of issue is irrelevant because the problem is not, "What result will I come up with?" If this were the relevant sense of the word, "issue", there could be no unsuccessful inquiry, for one will always come up with one result or another. That is, the problem for a hiker is not, "If I take this path what will happen?" If this were the problem and he presently found himself in the midst of a swamp or broke his leg before he had gone twenty yards, he should be quite happy because he had solved his inquiry. Such a sense of "issue" makes inquiry infallible and quite useless.

Rather, the problem is "Which path leads to safety?" or "Which path leads home?" Inquiry into this problem may be successful or unsuccessful. This, the second sense of the word, "issue", identifies the issue of an inquiry with the issue of successful inquiry, or what one might prefer to call simply the "answer to the problem". Is this the sense of "issue" that Dewey intends when he says that a situation is indeterminate in respect to its issue? If so, then his whole discussion of the indeterminate situation is subject to the charge of unintentional obfuscation of a rather ordinary observation, viz., that when one sets out to solve a problem he does not at the time know the answer.

Dewey goes on to make additional statements which explain the meaning of several synonyms of "indeterminate" in a manner similar to his explanation of "indeterminate". "If we call it *confused*, then it is meant that its outcome cannot be anticipated." [29] Does Dewey mean that the outcome of the situation cannot be anticipated by the inquirer? If so, then it is true, but trivial. Does he mean instead that the outcome cannot be anticipated by anyone? Then the statement is false. Again, he writes, "It is called *obscure* when its course of movement permits of final consequences that cannot be clearly made out." [30] Can no one make out the final consequences, or is it only that the inquirer cannot make them out? If the former, Dewey is simply wrong. If the latter, he is correct but is stating a commonplace in a manner suggesting a discovery. In the last of this series Dewey says, "It is called *conflicting* when it tends to evoke discordant

29   Dewey, *Logic*, p. 106.
30   Dewey, *Logic*, p. 106.

responses." [31] Does the situation tend to evoke discordant responses in everyone, or just in the one engaged in the inquiry? If the former, it is incorrect; if the latter, correct, but hardly the kind of answer the reader had a right to expect.

The principal charge against these explanations, then, is that they make the claim that the initial situation of inquiry is indeterminate either false or a commonplace. There is, however, another objection as well. The explanation furnished by these several parallel statements does not agree very well with the idea that the situation is inherently indeterminate, that we are doubtful because it is first doubtful, or that the doubtful character is not subjective. If an indeterminate situation is indeterminate because the inquirer does not know the issue of the inquiry, then it would seem better to say that the situation is indeterminate *with respect to* the inquirer. It is the very meaning of such a with-respect-to quality that it is not inherent in the situation. If doubtfulness is a with-respect-to quality, then it is simply false to hold that we are doubtful because the situation is doubtful. The order should be the other way around. Similarly, in a broad sense of "subjective" (meaning that the origin is in the person), it is also incorrect to say that the doubtful character of the situation is not subjective.

There is a way of understanding "indeterminate situation" that Dewey does not suggest, but which at first glance may seem to have some merit. One might be tempted to say that the initial situation of inquiry is indeterminate in those cases in which the results of the inquiry depend on which of several alternative actions the inquirer chooses. Thus, for example, a person who is lost in the woods and finds himself with four different paths to take might be described as facing an indeterminate situation because the outcome depends on which path he chooses.

The difficulty with this interpretation is that one never inquires into what he, himself, will choose. One may inquire into what he should do, or what he can do, or even, rarely, what he will do (when what he will do is not completely dependent on his choice), or what someone else will choose; but one does not inquire into what he, himself, will choose. Since the purpose of in-

[31] Dewey, *Logic*, p. 106.

quiry is to remove the indeterminacy from the situation and since one does not inquire into what he, himself, will choose, it follows that the indeterminacy of the initial situation is not due to the inquirer's not knowing what he will choose.

The argument might be restated in slightly different terms. If the outcome depends entirely on what the inquirer chooses, there would be no basis for inquiry. One may not know what he will choose; nevertheless, inquiry will not reveal it to him. To put it paradoxically, if inquiry does reveal it to him, he has already chosen. One may not know whether he will choose to vote in the next election, but whether he will choose to or not can hardly be a matter for inquiry for him. Of course, he may inquire whether he should vote, or whether he can; but these are different problems, problems whose outcomes are not wholly dependent on his choice. On the other hand, if the outcome depends only partly on what the inquirer chooses, then there is a basis for inquiry, but only to the extent that the outcome does not depend on his choice. The lost hiker who comes upon four paths is uncertain only to the extent of where each of the paths leads, and where they lead is not dependent on which he chooses. To put it differently, he is uncertain as to the outcome of the situation no matter which path he chooses, but the uncertainty is not based on which he chooses. The outcome is based on which path he chooses and the outcome is uncertain, but the outcome is not uncertain because it is based on which path he chooses.

Although the main purpose in this study is to understand Dewey and to evaluate what he says, and is not, generally speaking, to learn why he says what he does, there are times when knowing his reasons aids in understanding what he says. In the passage below he reveals why he attributes the characteristics of being doubtful, disturbed, etc. to the situation as inherent characteristics:

It is the *situation* that has these traits. *We* are doubtful because the situation is inherently doubtful. Personal states of doubt that are not evoked by and are not relative to some existential situation are pathological; when they are extreme they constitute the mania of doubting. Consequently, situations that are disturbed and troubled, confused or obscure, cannot be straightened out, cleared up and put in order, by manipulation of our personal states of mind. The attempt to settle them by such manipulations involves what psychiatrists call "withdrawal from reality". Such an attempt is pathological as far as it goes, and when it goes far it is the source of some form of actual insanity. The habit of disposing of the doubtful as if it belonged only to *us* rather than to the existential situation in which we are caught and implicated is an inheritance from subjectivistic psychology.[32]

There appear to be two distinct reasons why doubt, confusion, and the rest are presented as inherent properties of the situation. The first of these reasons is that personal states of doubt not evoked by some existential situation are pathological. The second is that if one says that a situation is not itself disturbed, he implies that a problem can be solved merely by the manipulation of one's state of mind. Let us consider each of these reasons separately.

Dewey offers the passage quoted above as a way of showing why one should accept his view that the situation is inherently doubtful, troubled, etc. When he says that personal states of doubt not evoked by some existential situation are pathological, he means to imply that if one does not adopt his view that situations are inherently doubtful, one must agree that the personal state of doubt is not evoked by anything existential. This means that the only thing Dewey allows as being "anything existential" is a doubtful situation. The only thing that Dewey admits as having the proper function of evoking a doubtful frame of mind is an inherently doubtful situation. It is clearly his intent that the other characteristics which he has found in the initial situation are to be treated in the same way. Perhaps he did not intend to speak of a "healthy confusion", a "healthy state of being troubled and disturbed", and a "healthy state of having conflicting tendencies", but these expressions are certainly implied. A person is not confused in a healthy sort of way unless the situation is first confused; he is not obscure in a healthy way unless the situation is obscure; and so on.

To hold such a view Dewey must espouse a curious sort of correspondence theory of doubt, a theory that reminds one of the

[32] Dewey, *Logic*, pp. 105-106.

correspondence theory of truth. Just as the correspondence theory of truth, in simplified form, says that a statement is true if and only if there is a corresponding fact, so also the correspondence theory of doubt says that a doubt is healthy if and only if there is a corresponding doubtful situation. In order for a person to be doubtful and not mentally sick, his doubt must represent or mirror a doubt in nature. One wonders why Dewey stopped where he did and why he did not go on to say that the situation is also inherently ignorant at the beginning of inquiry in order for the inquirer to be ignorant without being pathological. One criticism of Dewey's reasoning, therefore, is that it implies an absurd doctrine of a correspondence theory of doubt.

A second criticism pertains to Dewey's belief that if one does not agree that the situation is inherently doubtful, he is committed to the view that the personal state of doubt is not evoked by anything existential whatsoever. Suppose that while one is walking along the road to a certain village he comes upon a fork in the road. There are no signs to direct him, and he wonders which way he should go. He is in a state of doubt. It has been argued that Dewey is not very clear about what a situation is. Nevertheless, it must be something distinct from the inquirer, for he says that the inquirer is doubtful because the situation is doubtful. Since Dewey has also said that the initial situation is that which evokes inquiry, the initial situation, in this case, must be the fork in the road. In terms of this example, Dewey maintains that to say the fork in the road is not inherently doubtful is to say that the person's state of doubt is not evoked by anything existential. However, rejecting the view that the fork in the road is doubtful does not in any sense compel one to hold that one's doubt is not evoked by something real and existing. On the contrary, it is clear that since the man's doubt is evoked by the fork in the road, and since the fork in the road is quite obviously real and existing, his doubt is evoked by something existential.

There is also a second reason which Dewey offers for the view that the situation is inherently indeterminate, doubtful, etc. In the long passage quoted earlier, Dewey says, "Consequently, situations that are disturbed and troubled, confused or obscure, cannot be straightened out, cleared up and put in order, by manipulation of our personal states of mind." [33] Dewey feels, apparently, that if the situation were not itself doubtful, that is, if the doubt existed only in the inquirer, then problems would be solved simply by changing our attitudes and thoughts. By the phrase, "manipulation of our personal states of mind", presumably Dewey means adopting a new opinion, point of view, or attitude as a result of something other than demonstration and evidence. One is reminded of the art of persuasion, oratory designed to sway the multitude, commercial sales technique, and, of course, Plato's picture of the Sophists.

Consider the geologist endeavoring to identify a certain rock. The geologist is the inquirer. The rock is that which evokes the inquiry and so, presumably, is the initial situation. Ordinarily, we would say that the geologist is, at the beginning of this inquiry, doubtful about what kind of rock he sees; and, ordinarily, we would not describe the rock as being doubtful. Dewey, on the other hand, maintains that both are doubtful. He further maintains that if we do not acknowledge that the rock is doubtful, we are committed, whether we like it or not, to the view that the geologist can resolve his inquiry, i.e., identify the rock, by persuading himself that it is, say, gold rather than iron pyrites, such persuasion being a change in one's mental attitude. It is, however, incorrect to imply that the geologist is concerned only to remove his doubt. He is concerned not merely to remove his doubt, but to remove it by certain means. He is interested in removing his doubt by removing the reasons for the doubt. Although he could remove his doubt by taking a certain drug or by being hypnotized, he is simply not interested in these ways of removing doubt. Perhaps it would be more accurate to say that his aim is not to remove his doubt, but to solve his problem – and his problem is not that he doubts. His problem is to correctly identify a certain rock. The resolution of his inquiry is, of course, the correct identification of the rock, not the removal of his doubt. Removal of doubt is a psychological by-product of inquiry, but not its end.

[33] Dewey, *Logic*, p. 106.

II

THE DEVELOPING AND SOLVING OF A PROBLEM

In the first chapter we studied the antecedent conditions of inquiry. These antecedent conditions are the raw material, but as yet, as Dewey views it, there is no problem, no inquiry. "The unsettled or indeterminate situation might have been called a *problematic* situation. This name would have been, however, proleptic and anticipatory." [1] There is, therefore, good reason for calling indeterminate situations the "antecedent conditions" of inquiry. Dewey further distinguishes the indeterminate situation from the problem, itself, when he says that the indeterminate situation is something that happens to one, whereas the problem is something someone institutes. "The indeterminate situation comes into existence from existential causes, just as does, say, the organic imbalance of hunger." [2] "It is but an initial step in institution of a problem." [3]

Dewey here refers to the "institution of a problem". Saying that a problem is instituted seems to be contrasted with saying that a problem is formulated upon being recognized or with saying that a problem is articulated upon being discovered. It suggests that the reason why there is a problem at all depends on there being an inquirer who raises the problem.

In examining everyday situations, however, it seems apparent that not all problems are instituted. Some are, but most are not. To illustrate the latter first because they are more common, let us imagine a hunter returning to his cabin as twilight falls. He con-

[1]   John Dewey, *Logic: The Theory of Inquiry* (New York, 1938), p. 107.
[2]   Dewey, *Logic*, p. 107.
[3]   Dewey, *Logic*, p. 108.

fidently picks his way, certain that he knows where he is. For all his confidence, however, he is, let us suppose, quite lost. If one is lost, he has a problem; and if one is lost without realizing it, he has a problem without realizing it. Finally he tops a knoll and sees before him a lake where he expected to see his cabin. Only now does he recognize that he is lost. Only now, therefore, is he aware that he has a problem. The use of "recognize" is appropriate here because it implies that he had a problem before becoming aware of it. This problem was not dependent on the inquirer's awareness of it.

Now let us look at two examples of problems which do depend on the awareness of the person involved. Suppose that a person believes in ghosts and thinks that one is pursuing him. The problem, as he sees it, is that he is being pursued by a ghost. It would, however, not be a problem to him if he did not believe it. This was not so in the case of the lost hunter. He was lost whether he believed it or not. Of course, one might object to the ghost story on the grounds that since ghosts are unreal, the problem is an imaginary one, that an imaginary problem is not a real problem, and that something which is not a real problem is not a problem at all.

Here is another example to which such an irrelevant objection would not apply. Imagine a housewife who is to take a driver's test. She has had adequate practice and has learned the necessary skills. Nevertheless, she fears that she will make so many mistakes that she will not pass the test. When the awful moment arrives and she must prove her skill to the strangely silent officer, she does precisely what she feared she would do. As expressed from our point of view, the problem is that she fears she will make too many mistakes. From her point of view, it is simply that she will make too many mistakes. Her fear is a form of awareness. Her problem is real. Yet, it would not have been a problem had she not been aware of it. There are, no doubt, many such examples from the human scene where the fear of something makes that fear a well-grounded one, but this kind of problem is by no means so common as the kind which is independent of our awareness of it.

Dewey's reply, perhaps, would be that by saying that problems are instituted rather than discovered, it should have been clear that the first example offered is not applicable. That is, by saying that a problem is instituted rather than discovered, it should have been clear that the hunter does not have a problem until he becomes aware that he is lost. Were this Dewey's reply, it would merely mean victory by definition. As a matter of fact, we do talk about persons' being unaware of their problems, whereas in Dewey's scheme, such talk would be self-contradictory. To define "problem" so that problems are said to exist only when one becomes aware of them surely is a stipulative act. It introduces a quaint kind of idealism and would certainly supply the right philosophical underpinnings for the adage that ignorance is bliss.

Dewey seems, however, to protect himself from such criticisms by adding, "A problem is not a task to be performed which a person puts upon himself or that is placed upon him by others – like a so-called arithmetical 'problem' in school work. *A problem represents the partial transformation by inquiry of a problematic situation into a determinate situation.*" [4] However, if, as Dewey says, a problem is instituted by the person rather than discovered or recognized by him, one *would* think that the problem would be a task which the person puts upon himself. The answer presumably is that the person constructs the problem from the materials supplied by the indeterminate antecedent conditions. Although the problem is the result of something the inquirer does, it is not merely the result of something he does, since it is derived from that which is not the result of something he does, viz., the indeterminate situation. "On the other hand, to set up a problem that does not grow out of an actual situation is to start on a course of dead work, nonetheless dead because the work is 'busy work'." [5] The net result of this, however, is nothing more than to substitute the word, "problem", for the phrase, "formulation of a problem", and to substitute "antecedent conditions" and "indeterminate situation" (but not "problematic situation" since that, as we shall see later, involves a judgment) for "problem".

4   Dewey, *Logic*, p. 108.
5   Dewey, *Logic*, p. 108.

As usual, switching words, whether intentionally or, as Dewey seems to have done, unintentionally, accomplishes nothing. Other words must be borrowed or coined to convey the old meanings. If problems do not exist until instituted and, consequently, we now are to use "problem" where we formerly used "formulation of a problem" or "articulation of a problem" or "awareness of a problem", then we need a new general expression to describe such things as the lost hunter while he was unaware that he was lost. Instead of saying that he has a problem, we might now decide to say that he has trouble. He has trouble, but no problem. Of course, as soon as he learns that he is lost, then he has both trouble and a problem. The word, "trouble", now performs part of the work previously done by "problem"; consequently, "trouble" is used a little more frequently, "problem" a little less frequently. Nothing more is accomplished. The world has not changed, nor is our understanding of it deepened.

Since Dewey does, nevertheless, hold that all problems are instituted, the next question is, "What is the first step in the institution of a problem?" Dewey writes, "The first result of evocation of inquiry is that the situation is taken, adjudged, to be problematic. To see that a situation requires inquiry is the initial step in inquiry." [6] He also says, "Qualification of a situation as problematic does not, however, carry inquiry far. It is but an initial step in institution of a problem." [7] The institution of a problem begins with recognizing *that* there is a problem. Presumably, then, the problem, itself, is not recognized until later. Is it, however, always the case that before the problem, itself, is recognized, one judges that there is a problem? Let us first take the obvious interpretation that when Dewey says that the situation is judged to be problematic, he means the judging as a temporal event that actually happens. In the example of the physician and the sick man, suppose that the doctor first heard of the case when the patient reported a pain in the stomach. This is as far back as one can go in this inquiry. There are no previous stages. Yet, upon receiving the call the doctor is immediately aware of the problem,

[6] Dewey, *Logic*, p. 107.
[7] Dewey, *Logic*, p. 108.

itself, and is never aware of only the aspect that there is a problem.

It is true, of course, that there sometimes is awareness of only the problematic nature of something. The doctor may have been given a mixed list of symptoms; but, because of many previous calls from the same patient about imagined maladies, he did not at first think that the person was ill. However, as he looks over the list, the thought occurs that there is a problem. A moment later he can articulate it. Such cases are less frequent than those in which there is no separate stage of being aware only that there is a problem.

When Dewey speaks of the first step of inquiry as being the judging that the situation is problematic, is it possible that he is not referring to a temporal stage at all? Would he, perhaps, acknowledge that one frequently cannot actually point to the first step or time it with a stop watch, but still insist that it is there in another, a non-temporal sense? It is quite common to speak of thinking, judging, seeing, and the like in other than a temporal sense. Thus, for example, if, while coming downstairs, one misses the bottom step, he might say that he thought there were no more steps. Yet no one would suppose that he meant he had consciously thought this. It would seem, therefore, that Dewey might not mean that there is a conscious, temporal act even though he says that the situation is judged to be problematic.

There is, nevertheless, a strong reason for saying that this is not the sense of "judge" that Dewey intends when he says that a situation is judged to be problematic. Note that in this same sense there are countless things the person coming downstairs could be said to judge. He could be said to judge that the second to the last step was really there, that the third to the last was not made of rubber, that the fourth to the last step was built when the others were built, etc. In this sense of "judge" there seems to be no end to the number of things one could be said to judge while descending the stairs. Is it in this sense that Dewey speaks when he says that the situation is judged to be problematic? Presumably not, for if it were, Dewey would have had no reason for listing only this judgement. There would have been numerous other judgments with equal claim for mention; for example, he might have mentioned that the situation will continue to exist, that the situation is either problematic or not, that the items in the situation are really here, that the situation is temporally related to other situations, etc. Since judgments in this sense are rather uninteresting, it seems likely that Dewey meant judgment in the sense in which it is a conscious and temporal act. It has already been shown, however, that in this sense it is not the case that inquiry always begins with the judgment that the situation is problematic. In the sense that Dewey must have meant, what he said is factually false.

The judgment that the situation is problematic is followed, predictably, by the statement of the problem. Dewey writes, "Statement of a problematic situation in terms of a problem has no meaning save as the problem instituted has, in the very terms of its statement, reference to a possible solution." [8] In order to prevent the statement of a problem from being meaningless, and, hence, not a statement of a problem at all, one must be sure that the statement refers to a possible solution. How does one state a problem so that it has reference to a possible solution? Perhaps one could first state the problem, for example, "How can I get my car out of the snow drift?" and then add, "Perhaps chains will do it." This, however, is doing considerably more than stating a problem. It is both stating a problem and offering a solution.

In the next sentence Dewey seems to explain himself: "Just because a problem well stated is on its way to solution . . ." [9] This passage suggests that in order to state a problem in such a way that its possible solution is referred to, one must state a problem well. The next sentence reads, "If we assume, prematurely, that the problem involved is definite and clear, subsequent inquiry proceeds on the wrong track." [10] If there is continuity of thought paralleling the continuity of sentences, this sentence should be related to the preceding one about a well-stated problem. Presumably, then, a well-stated problem is one which is definite and

8   Dewey, *Logic*, p. 108.
9   Dewey, *Logic*, p. 108.
10 Dewey, *Logic*, p. 108.

clear. This is a reasonable enough claim. However, following the usual meanings of "definite" and "clear", there surely is no connection between saying that a meaningful statement of a problem refers to its solution and saying that it is definite and clear. Dewey goes on to give his own meaning. For context the previous quotation is repeated: "If we assume, prematurely, that the problem involved is definite and clear, subsequent inquiry proceeds on the wrong track. Hence the question arises: How is the formation of a genuine problem so controlled that further inquiries will move toward a solution?" [11] If the second sentence is taken as shedding light on the first, as well as carrying the thought further, then it turns out that a problem which is definite and clear is one whose further inquiries move toward a solution. The first objection is similar to the objection above; viz., there is no apparent connection between the statement of a problem which refers to a solution and one whose further inquiries move toward a solution.

Furthermore, the passage merely raises the question of what Dewey means by further inquiries. Does he mean later stages of the same inquiry, or does he mean subsequent complete inquiries? If the latter, we must remember that Dewey is explaining the structure of all inquiry. The account which he gives of the first or main inquiry must also be the account of all subsequent inquiry. This means that each subsequent inquiry requires subsequent inquiry of its own. Since any given inquiry generates an infinite series of subsequent inquiries if it is to be completed, it can never be completed.

On the other hand, by "subsequent inquiry" Dewey might mean, and very probably does mean, later stages of the first inquiry. Admittedly, it is somewhat unusual to talk about later stages of an inquiry as inquiries. Nevertheless, if this is what he means, then "meaningful statement of a problem", "problem which refers to its solution", "well-stated problem", "definite and clear problem" all refer to a problem whose subsequent stages do not go astray, i.e., a problem which does, in fact, get solved.

It surely is unusual to explain what a well-stated problem is in

[11]   Dewey, *Logic*, p. 108.

terms of things that occur after the problem is stated. This is quite different from explaining what a well-stated problem is on the basis of criteria present when the problem is formulated and then adding the sound advice that a problem stated well is more likely to end in a successful solution than one that is stated poorly. In any event, since a meaningful statement of a problem is said to be one whose subsequent inquiry (i.e., later stages) is successful, it becomes crucial to ask with Dewey, "How is the formation of a genuine problem so controlled that further inquiries will move toward a solution?"

Dewey answers the question by describing the procedural details of this stage of inquiry, that is, by describing the methodology of formulating and solving the problem. Let us first sketch them, then evaluate them as an answer, and finally use them as a point of departure for the topic of Dewey's doctrine of ideas and his doctrine of facts.

Dewey writes, "The first step in answering this question is to recognize that no situation which is *completely* indeterminate can possibly be converted into a problem having definite constituents. The first step then is to search out the *constituents* of a given situation which, as constituents, are settled." [12] Dewey is saying simply that one must note whatever relevant facts he can find before going on to formulate the problem. The example he gives is that of a fire in an assembly hall. The problem, of course, is how to escape. The first task is to observe where the fire is, where the aisles and exits are located, in what direction the people are moving, etc.

The second step is to devise a possible solution. "A *possible* relevant solution is then suggested by the determination of factual conditions which are secured by observation. The possible solution presents itself, therefore, as an *idea*, just as the terms of the problem (which are facts) are instituted by observation." [13] Dewey emphasizes, and rightly so, that the solution is suggested by the observed facts.

The third step is the interaction between the facts and the pro-

[12]   Dewey, *Logic*, pp. 108-109.
[13]   Dewey, *Logic*, p. 109.

posed solution. Dewey correctly notes that a proposed solution has an influence on which additional facts are observed. It often leads to the observation of facts previously not noticed. Similarly, these newly observed facts may suggest another solution. Ideas of a possible solution lead to new observations, and new observations lead to still other possible solutions. "Observation of facts and suggested meanings or ideas arise and develop in correspondence with each other." [14] So much for the sketch of the procedure of inquiry.

We must remember that Dewey gives these three steps as an answer to the question, "How is the formation of a genuine problem so controlled that further inquiries will move toward a solution?" There are two objections to his answer. The first objection is that Dewey's outline of the procedure of inquiry does not at all guarantee that further inquiry will move toward a solution. It is just good general advice on how to conduct inquiry. Furthermore, we must remember that the foregoing explanations are supposed to make it clear what Dewey means when he says that a meaningful statement of a problem is one which refers to a possible solution. The answer Dewey gives turns out to be wholly irrelevant to that question. The question talks about how a problem is stated; the answer talks about how, once you have a problem, you go about solving it.

Dewey describes the formulation of the problem as a gradual, continuing affair, proceeding by degrees. That is, as he looks at it, the original problem is replaced by others, each succeeding version being an improvement on those preceding. It is true that there often are successive reformulations of a problem. There are, however, two objections to what Dewey claims. The first is that he is wrong in implying that there is a successive reformulation going on in every inquiry. He evidently has in mind the great experiments in science and has forgotten the small and common place inquiries which fill our lives. The second objection is that it is incorrect to hold, with respect to those cases in which there is reformulation, that these always replace the original problem.

[14] Dewey, *Logic*, p. 109.

They may or may not, depending on how broadly the problem was originally formulated. Let us suppose that the physician is confronted with the symptoms of a headache, nausea, and a slight rash. He may formulate his problem simply, "What causes this man's headache, nausea, and rash?" Upon further examination he learns that the patient also has a fever. Now he reformulates the problem into, "What causes this man's headache, nausea, rash, and fever?" This would be a case in which the reformulation replaces the original problem. (No distinction is being drawn between "reformulation of a problem" and "different problem". On some occasions these expressions are, no doubt, used differently, but then the context makes this clear.) On the other hand, the physician may first address himself to the more general problem, "Why is this man ill?" There follows the more specific problem, "What causes his headache, nausea, and rash?" and the reformulation of it, "What causes his headache, nausea, rash, and fever?" In this case, however, the original problem, "Why is this man ill?" is not replaced. Whether or not a new formulation replaces the original problem depends, therefore, on how broadly the original problem was formulated.

We began this chapter by looking at Dewey's statements to the effect that inquiry proper and the institution of the problem begin with the judgment that a situation is problematic. Under close examination this doctrine withered and died. The next topic, the formulation of the problem, itself, was one about which a fruitful discussion could certainly have been expected. Although there undoubtedly are things to say about the formulation of a problem which are good and true and, moreover, intelligible, Dewey elected to remain obscure so that, with one exception, his remarks have netted nothing. This exception is his outline of the procedure of inquiry. We recall that in this outline Dewey stated that after determinate features of the indeterminate situation have been noted, the inquirer proposes a solution to the problem. This Dewey calls an "idea" and in the course of explaining it, develops a rather complete, but also an unusual doctrine of ideas. It is to this doctrine of ideas that we now turn.

A. IDEAS

Ideas play a vital role in Dewey's understanding of inquiry, and in the course of describing this role he develops an interesting and highly controversial doctrine of ideas generally. The account begins innocently enough: "The possible solution presents itself, therefore, as an *idea*, just as the terms of the problem (which are facts) are instituted by observation." [15] This passage need not be controversial since by itself it can be taken as a somewhat unusual way of saying that one *thinks* of the possible solution just as one *observes* the terms of the problem.

Dewey proceeds, "Ideas are anticipated consequences (forecasts) of what will happen when certain operations are executed under and with respect to observed conditions." [16] One might read this passage as saying that the ideas are the anticipated consequences, but are not about the operations which lead to them. This impression is corrected in the following passage: "One kind of operations deals with ideational or conceptual subject-matter. This subject-matter stands for possible ways and ends of resolution." [17] One could wish for a little more accord between these excerpts. Instead, however, of saying that Dewey contradicts himself, it is perhaps better to say that he holds that ideas are both solutions and the operations which lead to them.

It is not controversial to say that a suggested operation and its anticipated consequence are an idea. What is controversial is saying it the other way around, that ideas are suggested operations and their consequences. This phrasing suggests that all ideas are suggested operations and their consequences, that there are no ideas which are not of operations and their consequences. It suggests that there are no ideas which are not proposed solutions to problems. That this is, indeed, what Dewey means is supported by a statement he makes later in a totally different context: "A strictly *possible* operation constitutes an idea or conception." [18]

[15] Dewey, *Logic*, p. 109.
[16] Dewey, *Logic*, p. 109.
[17] Dewey, *Logic*, p. 117.
[18] Dewey, *Logic*, p. 289.

In a long and interesting footnote Dewey discloses that he intends his statement to describe all ideas, that he is, in fact, defining the word, "idea".

The theory of *ideas* that has been held in psychology and epistemology since the time of Locke's successors is completely irrelevant and obstructive in logical theory. For in treating them as copies of perceptions or "impressions", it ignores the prospective and anticipatory character that defines *being* an idea. Failure to define ideas functionally, in the reference they have to a solution of a problem, is one reason they have been treated as merely "mental". The notion, on the other hand, that ideas are fantasies is a derivative. Fantasies arise when the function an idea performs is ruled out when it is entertained and developed.[19]

One wonders whether Dewey thought of himself as defining the word, "idea", or as redefining it. He was actually redefining it, for he gives it a range more limited than usage accords. If one were to follow Dewey's definition of "idea" in which an idea, any idea, is a proposed solution to a problem, one could not speak of the "idea of democracy", of a "book being full of ideas", or of the "idea I had yesterday at lunch", and so on, because such ideas, at least usually, are not proposed solutions to problems. For example, one may remark to a companion while one is engaged in idle conversation (which could not be construed as inquiry) that people seem nowadays to be obsessed with the idea of speed. This reference to an idea is not a reference to a proposed solution of a problem. Dewey, however, would have to rule out such a use of "idea". One could speak only of his idea of a solution to a specific problem. It seems strange that Dewey should choose to define the word in such a restricted way. The result is only to make necessary another word to carry the additional meanings now carried by "idea". One would be obliged then to speak of the "notion of democracy", or of a "book being full of concepts", or, perhaps, one would have to coin an entirely new word.

Dewey is, moreover, inconsistent in the matter. In the following three passages, he uses "conception" and "idea" as synonyms:

Observation of facts and suggested meanings or ideas arise and devel-

19 Dewey, *Logic*, p. 109.

op in correspondence with each other. The more the facts of the case come to light in consequence of being subjected to observation, the clearer and more pertinent become the conceptions of the way the problem constituted by these facts is to be dealt with.[20]

In logical fact, perceptual and conceptual materials are instituted in functional correlativity with each other, in such a manner that the former locates and describes the problem while the latter represents a possible method of solution.[21]

The transition is achieved by means of operations of two kinds which are in functional correspondence with each other. One kind of operations deals with ideational or conceptual subject-matter.[22]

The point of showing that Dewey uses "idea" and "conception" synonymously is that although Dewey defines "idea" as a proposed solution, he does, on occasion, use "conception" in a way in which it is not a proposed solution. This he does in the following: "Any account of, say, the assassination of Julius Caesar assuredly involves the generic conceptions of assassination, conspiracy, political ambition, human beings, of which it is an exemplifying case and it cannot be reported and accounted for without the use of such general conceptions."[23] Certain concepts are mentioned as occurring in the account of the assassination of Caesar. An account is, of course, a description. Now descriptions may be used for all sorts of purposes. It is true that they may be used to describe a proposed solution to a problem, but their use is certainly not limited to that. For example, a description may be used to state the problem, or it may be used outside the context of inquiry entirely. When Dewey acknowledges that concepts occur in descriptions, he, by implication, also acknowledges that concepts are not proposed solutions only. Since a concept and an idea are one and the same, he implies that ideas are not proposed solutions only. Therefore, he is inconsistent.

The difference between these two kinds of ideas is amplified in how each is expressed in language. Dewey has described ideas

[20] Dewey, *Logic*, p. 109.
[21] Dewey, *Logic*, p. 111.
[22] Dewey, *Logic*, p. 117.
[23] Dewey, *Logic*, p. 501.

as being proposed solutions to problems. Such ideas are usually stated in full sentences; or, if they are not, the expressions are clearly elliptical. The solution to the physician's problem might be, for example, "The patient has indigestion." In the last passage quoted, however, Dewey has an entirely different kind of thing in mind when he speaks of concepts of assassination, of conspiracy, of political ambition, and so on. He is here speaking of that which is expressed in single words or short phrases, never in complete sentences.

Earlier a long footnote was quoted containing Dewey's criticism of Locke's account of ideas. At that point the footnote was used to show that Dewey regards the statement that an idea is a proposed solution as a definition. Since the footnote is also of interest in its own right, let us take a closer look at several of its claims. One of these claims is that an idea is not a copy of a perception or an impression. Another is that an idea is to be defined functionally, that is, in terms of what it does. An additional one is that the function of an idea has reference to something in the future, that it has a "prospective and anticipatory character" about it. Still another is that ideas are not "merely mental". The last one is that ideas are not fantasies.

The first claim is that an idea is not a copy of a perception or an impression because it has an anticipatory character about it. It is true that Locke may not have defined "idea" very well. The reason which Dewey gives why Locke's definition is inadequate is not, however, a good one. Locke defined "idea" in terms of the source of an idea. Dewey defines it in terms of its use. There is no apparent reason why one method is to be preferred over the other. If Dewey knew of such a reason, he should have stated it. What he has stated is only that Locke's definition is wrong because it does not state the function of an idea, but he has not stated why a definition which omits function is wrong.

One might object to a definition because it does not go far enough. Such a definition would be described as "inadequate" or "incomplete" and would be, therefore, a poor definition. On the other hand, one might object to a definition, not because it is incomplete, but because what it says is incorrect. If one defines "bird" as a vehicle running on four wheels capable of carrying passengers, the definition would be wrong in this latter sense. Dewey regards Locke's definition as wrong in this sense. He regards it as simply incorrect to say that ideas are copies of impressions and sensations. Furthermore, he thinks that by revealing Locke's failure to mention the function of an idea, he has shown that ideas are not copies of impressions and sensations. Far from showing anything of the sort, his comment does not even serve as evidence. Things have both a source and a function. Showing that one has omitted the function does not prove that he has misdescribed the source.

The second claim found in the footnote is that an idea is to be defined functionally, that is, in terms of what it does. Dewey appears to give this as a general principle of definitions. The two sentences of that footnote which suggest this interpretation are these: "For in treating them as copies of perceptions or 'impressions', it ignores the prospective and anticipatory character that defines *being* an idea. Failure to define ideas functionally, in the reference they have to a solution of a problem, is one reason they have been treated as merely 'mental'." [24] It should not, however, be thought of as an innovation on Dewey's part that functionalism is important in definitions. Functionalism in definitions is probably as old as definitions. The word, "hammer", could scarcely be defined without reference to the use of a hammer. Dewey, however, appears to mean that all definitions are to be functional and that they are to be wholly functional. This seems to be a principle which is not only rash, but one which is impossible to carry out if one is to have adequate definitions. A functional definition of "chair" would be something like, "A chair is what one sits on." This definition would, however, not differentiate a chair from a stool, a sofa, or even on occasion a bed, the floor, or a stump. The ultimate criterion of a definition is whether or not it enables one to use the word correctly when occasion demands. A functional definition of "chair" does not meet this criterion. Nor would it help matters to any great extent

[24]   Dewey, *Logic*, p. 109.

to describe the function of a chair more fully, for there is no function that a chair can perform which something else cannot also perform.

Although Dewey's remarks about the necessity of defining "idea" in terms of the function of an idea have been taken as being about all definitions, such an extension could conceivably be challenged. Dewey frequently suggests a highly controversial notion, then leaves a lingering doubt concerning whether he really means it. If, however, one were to insist that Dewey does not speak for all definitions, it would mean that he only holds some, but not all, definitions to be wholly functional. If he holds this, it is, of course, correct and is not at all controversial.

The next and third claim of the footnote quoted earlier is that the function of an idea has reference to something in the future, that it has a "prospective and anticipatory character" about it. It seems that Dewey has taken a bad idea, the idea that all definitions describe functions, and made the worst of it by putting unreasonable restraints on the type of functions to be allowed. He allows reference to the future use of a thing, but not to its present or past use. The objection here, as it was above, is that Dewey is needlessly restricting what it is to define something.

The fourth claim is that ideas are not merely "mental". Does Dewey mean that they are mental, but not only mental? Or does he mean that they are not mental at all? We will look first at the interpretation that they are not mental at all.

Earlier we saw that Dewey means "idea" and "conception" to be synonyms. In fact, he maintains their synonymy throughout the book. Conceptions, however, have always been regarded as something having to do with thinking. It is true, of course, that, like ideas, conceptions are not always mental. We sometimes use the words, "concept" and "conception", in contexts other than those in which there is reference to mental activity. For example, we might note that the concept of world peace is much in the news these days. We do not mean that a certain kind of mental event is in the news. Yet, at the same time, the notion of certain mental events, of certain thoughts and awarenesses, is lingering backstage. The concept of world peace would not be in the news unless people had been thinking about world peace. Since Dewey uses "conception" in its customary way, and uses "idea" as a synonym, he ought not to have said that ideas are not "merely mental" if he means that they are not mental at all.

Dewey has also said, "Ideas are anticipated consequences (forecasts) of what will happen when certain operations are executed under and with respect to observed conditions." [25] If Dewey means that ideas are not mental at all, does he mean that these operations and consequences can be anticipated and predicted in some other way than by means of thinking? If so, he should have explained this method, for that would indeed have been worth writing about. If not, then he should not have said ideas are not merely mental except in the unexciting sense that they are mental and more, for to think is to do something mental.

Here are two passages which, like the one above, are incomprehensible unless they are understood in the context of thinking as a mental activity: "Because suggestions and ideas are of that which is not present in given existence . . ." [26] "Observed facts in their office of locating and describing the problem are existential; ideational subject-matter is non-existential." [27] All this would be quite mysterious if we did not know very well that Dewey is talking about the very common and very familiar everyday experience of thinking. He writes as if he had some new insight into the nature of ideas, but, in reality, since he has redefined "idea" so that an idea is an anticipated solution, he is making the trivial statement that an anticipated solution is a solution not yet present. In the second quotation above about ideational subject matter being non-existential, he is surely referring to the thought of a solution. Dewey has not even begun to get rid of the mental element in the concept of ideas.

Dewey also speaks of reasoning in respect to ideas. Reasoning, however, has generally been regarded as rigorous or logical thinking, and, as a kind of thinking, hence a mental process.

The second interpretation of the claim that ideas are not mere-

---

[25] Dewey, *Logic*, p. 109.
[26] Dewey, *Logic*, p. 110.
[27] Dewey, *Logic*, p. 112.

ly mental is that ideas are mental, but more besides. Since we speak both of thinking of ideas and of ideas that are in books (to give only two kinds of usage), it is obvious that ideas are mental, but more besides. This view, however, is the common one and is inappropriate to the controversial manner in which Dewey speaks.

The last claim found in the footnote quoted earlier is that ideas are not fantasies. It is surprising to find Dewey talking about fantasies because fantasies are usually thought of as ideas, thoughts, beliefs which are not true, and Dewey, as is known well, rejects the traditional notion of truth and falsity. It is also surprising because we ordinarily do not view ideas *per se* as fantasies. Furthermore, no major philosopher ever has, with the possible exception of Berkeley. (Even the case of Berkeley is debatable because within the terms of his system he distinguished between fantasy and true ideas.) Locke, whom Dewey seems to imagine here as his opponent, never thought ideas as such were fantasies.

Let us now leave the footnote and turn to new material on Dewey's concept of an idea. Having said at some length that an idea is a possible solution to a problem, Dewey now says that not all possible solutions are ideas. Some are what he calls "suggestions". "Every idea originates as a suggestion, but not every suggestion is an idea. The suggestion becomes an idea when it is examined with reference to its functional fitness; its capacity as a means of resolving the given situation." [28]

It is a little confusing to the reader to learn that what he had just been told are ideas now perhaps are not. We can no longer say confidently that an idea is a possible solution. The new definition must be that an idea is a possible solution which has been examined in respect to its capacity to resolve a given situation; or, to put it more simply, an idea is an examined possible solution. An unexamined one is a suggestion. This raises the question of how the examination of the suggestion is to be conducted, for it would seem that a suggested solution could not be adequately examined in respect to its capacity to resolve a given situation without acting on that suggestion. This would mean that a suggestion

[28]   Dewey, *Logic*, p. 110.

does not become an idea unless it is in fact tried as the solution. Dewey, however, corrects this impression.

This examination takes the form of reasoning, as a result of which we are able to appraise better than we were at the outset, the pertinency and weight of the meaning now entertained with respect to its functional capacity. But the final test of its possession of these properties is determined when it actually functions – that is, when it is put into operation so as to institute by means of observations facts not previously observed, and is then used to organize them with other facts into a coherent whole.[29]

The best reading of this passage seems to be that the examination which raises suggestions to the level of ideas is just the first part, the part which is limited to reasoning.

Introducing a new aspect of his doctrine of ideas, Dewey continues, "Because suggestions and ideas are of that which is not present in given existence, the meanings which they involve must be embodied in some symbol. Without some kind of symbol no idea; a meaning that is completely disembodied can not be entertained or used." [30] The reasoning in these lines seems excessively illusive. Let us suppose that the problem is to get one's automobile out of a snow drift and that a possible and examined solution is to use chains. The proposal to use chains is, therefore, an idea. When Dewey says, "Because suggestions and ideas are of that which is not present in given existence . . .", he would be referring, in terms of the example, to the stage when one is not yet using chains. He then adds that without some kind of symbol the idea cannot be entertained. Before we can finish the argument, we need to know what Dewey means by "symbol". "Since an existence (which *is* an existence) is the support and vehicle of a meaning and is a symbol instead of a merely physical existence only in this respect . . ." [31] A symbol is something physical. Dewey undoubtedly has words, both written and spoken, especially in mind, although elsewhere he makes it clear that he does not limit symbols to language. However, since in practice the symbols favored

29   Dewey, *Logic*, p. 110.
30   Dewey, *Logic*, p. 110.
31   Dewey, *Logic*, p. 110.

are those of language, the question reduces to whether or not one can think about using chains without talking aloud, whispering to himself, or writing himself notes. Obviously one can, and obviously Dewey is quite wrong when he says that because ideas are of that which is not present, they must be embodied in some symbol.

There is another puzzling statement in the latter part of the paragraph from which the last quotation was taken. Beginning with the above quotation for context, it reads, "Since an existence (which *is* an existence) is the support and vehicle of a meaning and is a symbol instead of a merely physical existence only in this respect, embodied meanings or ideas are capable of objective survey and development. To 'look at an idea' is not a mere literary figure of speech." [32] Dewey says that since a symbol of an idea is something physical, ideas are open to objective survey and one can literally look at them. There is, of course, one interpretation which is not controversial at all. One might mean only that, for example, since books are full of ideas, since the symbols of these ideas are ink marks, since ink marks are physical things, and since physical things are capable of objective survey, therefore ideas are capable of objective survey. It is not, however, a very novel idea to say that ideas are capable of objective survey if one only means that written words are capable of being seen. Undoubtedly, Dewey means more. Indeed, in the interpretation just given, it is not literally the idea that is objectively observed, but the marks.

The only other way to read Dewey is to take him at his word; that is, when he says ideas can literally be looked at, that we take him to mean just that. What he says, then, becomes absurd because we can see only things physically present and ideas, following Dewey's own meaning of the word, "idea", are not physically present. The reason offered why ideas can be seen, viz., because the symbol is a physically existing thing, is simply irrelevant since Dewey is talking about looking at the idea and is not talking about looking at the symbol.

[32] Dewey, *Logic*, p. 110.

B. REASONING

Dewey gives considerable emphasis to the part reasoning plays in the operation of ideation. He explains what reasoning is as follows:

The necessity of developing the meaning-contents of ideas in their relations to one another has been incidentally noted. This process, operating with symbols (constituting propositions) is reasoning in the sense of ratiocination or rational discourse . . . This examination consists in noting what the meaning in question implies in relation to other meanings in the system of which it is a member, the formulated relation constituting a proposition.[33]

It is interesting to note that Dewey limits reasoning to reasoning by means of propositions. This is a considerable limitation, for it excludes the use of words and phrases which are not propositions, the use of images, and any other possibilities. If one were talking about the communication of reasoning from one person to another, then it seems permissible to limit reasoning to propositions so long as one makes allowance for mathematical reasoning. Dewey, however, is talking about reasoning *per se*, which must then include reasoning which is not communicated to another. It is probably impossible to settle the question of how people in fact go about reasoning, especially so long as introspection is out of style, but it seems a little hasty to banish all non-propositional forms without a hearing.

In the passage last quoted Dewey explains reasoning as the working out of the implications of an idea. He finds two purposes for reasoning. Concerning the first purpose, he writes, "Through a series of intermediate meanings, a meaning is finally reached which is more clearly *relevant* to the problem in hand than the originally suggested idea. It indicates operations which can be performed to test its applicability, whereas the original idea is usually too vague to determine crucial operations." [34] One purpose of reasoning, according to this selection, is to reach a form of the suggested solution which is clearer and easier to test than was the

33 Dewey, *Logic*, p. 111.
34 Dewey, *Logic*, pp. 111-112.

original form. It is easy enough in the history of science to find examples in which the implications had to be worked out from the original hypothesis in order to test that hypothesis. The suggestion that all reasoning is used to this end, however, is preposterous. One exception which readily comes to mind is the use of reasoning, not to get an implication that is more easily tested, but to get the answer, itself, as is done in mathematics or in the solving of a deductive problem.

Reasoning, Dewey allows, has also another purpose, a purpose related to the one described above. This purpose is to prevent inquiry from being completed too quickly. "When a suggested meaning is immediately accepted, inquiry is cut short. Hence the conclusion reached is not grounded, even if it happens to be correct. The check upon immediate acceptance is the examination of the meaning as a meaning." [35] Since truth and grounded conclusions will be the subject of a later chapter, there is perhaps little to be said at this point except to make the general observation that Dewey seems to overestimate the importance of going through the process of inquiry and to underestimate the importance of a correct conclusion.

Finally, Dewey adds that in familiar situations reasoning may be no longer needed. "In many familiar situations, the meaning that is most relevant has been settled because of the eventuations of experiments in prior cases so that it is applicable almost immediately upon its occurrence." [36] According to this passage it is not necessary to reason in each inquiry because the most relevant and most testable implication of the possible solution has already been settled by a previous inquiry.

C. FACTS

Within inquiry there are two operations which act in conjunction with each other. The one has to do with ideas and reasoning, and this we have already examined. The other has to do with the ob-

[35]   Dewey, *Logic*, p. 111.
[36]   Dewey, *Logic*, p. 112.

servation of facts. Dewey has described each operation as being correlative to the other. Each affects the other. An idea of a possible solution leads to new observations, and new observations lead to modification of the idea, while reason acts as a method of making it easier for the idea to be tested.

Although there is interaction between observation of facts and ideas, observation starts the process. "The first step then is to search out the *constituents* of a given situation which, as constituents, are settled." [37] Then comes the interaction between observation and ideation. "Observation of facts and suggested meanings or ideas arise and develop in correspondence with each other." [38]

Dewey sometimes refers to facts as "the facts of the case" or "the terms of the problem". He is not consistent in this matter, however. On one occasion, as he is illustrating the remark that observation forms the first step of this stage of inquiry with an example of a fire in an assembly hall, he writes, "All of these observed conditions taken together constitute 'the facts of the case'. They constitute the terms of the problem, because they are conditions that must be reckoned with or taken account of in any relevant solution that is proposed." [39] The terms of the problem are quite plainly nothing more than the observed facts. There is no mention of facts which at first appear to be among those which set the problem, but which later do not. A few pages later, however, Dewey changes course. "Meantime, the orders of fact, which present themselves in consequence of the experimental observations the ideas call out and direct, are *trial* facts. They are provisional. They are 'facts' if they are observed by sound organs and techniques. But they are not on that account the *facts of the case*." [40] The new requirement is that in order to be facts of the case, they must serve as evidence. "They are tested or 'proved' with respect to their evidential function just as much as ideas (hypotheses) are tested with reference to their power to exercise the function of resolution." [41]

[37] Dewey, *Logic*, pp. 108-109.
[38] Dewey, *Logic*, p. 109.
[39] Dewey, *Logic*, p. 109.
[40] Dewey, *Logic*, p. 114.
[41] Dewey, *Logic*, p. 114.

We have, then, two different explanations of what are to be considered the facts of the case. Perhaps it would be overstrict to say that Dewey is involved in another contradiction. It would be more fair to regard the second explanation as a further qualification of the first, though it might be added that Dewey's way of presenting the matter could bear improvement.

In talking about ideas, Dewey stated that, because that which ideas are of is not present, ideas must have physical symbols to be entertained. Observed facts, however, are present, so one would expect that they would not need symbols in order to be used. Instead, Dewey argues that facts as well as ideas must have symbols attached to them. The reason is as follows:

Observed facts, on the other hand, are existentially present. It might seem therefore, that symbols are not required for referring to them. But if they are not carried and treated by means of symbols, they lose their provisional character, and in losing this character they are categorically asserted and inquiry comes to an end. The carrying on of inquiry requires that the facts be taken as *repre*-sentative and not just as *pre*-sented. This demand is met by formulating them in propositions – that is, by means of symbols. Unless they are so represented they relapse into the total qualitative situation.[42]

The first two sentences do not pose a problem in understanding, but the third does. In the third sentence Dewey says that if observed facts are not "carried and treated by means of symbols, they lose their provisional character, and in losing this character they are categorically asserted and inquiry comes to an end". Unfortunately, there seems to be no justification at all for this intriguing view. When a person puts together a jigsaw puzzle, he does not name or describe the pieces. He may, at times, mutter, "Will that piece fit?" or "There's the one I'm looking for", but he also might try piece after piece, gradually fitting in the right ones, and do this with no words either spoken aloud or formulated in thought. If putting a jigsaw puzzle together is an example of inquiry, and there is no apparent reason why it should not be, then, presumably, the various pieces would be among the terms of

42   Dewey, *Logic*, p. 114.

the problem. It is a little more difficult, however, to understand what "asserting a fact" would mean in terms of this example. Perhaps it would mean either that the inquirer asserts that these various pieces are terms of the problem, which in this case would mean that they belong to the puzzle, or that this particular piece goes in this particular place. Under either interpretation the inquirer can refuse to assert the facts and do so without using symbols. He might toss one piece aside as not belonging to the rest of the puzzle, or he might toss one aside as not being the right one to fit in a certain place, and do either without a word. On the other hand, he might talk about each piece as he picks it up and, for some reason (for example, poor eyesight), believe it to be the right one. Using language is not necessary for either asserting or not asserting a fact.

Furthermore, suppose Dewey were granted his point that the symbolization of a fact prevents its assertion. There is no stage in Dewey's version of inquiry when the use of propositions ceases. Indeed, as we shall see in the next chapter, the conclusion of inquiry is a judgment expressed in a proposition whose subject is said to be the facts of the case. There seems to be a difficulty here. If the use of symbols in respect to facts continues throughout inquiry and if the use of symbols prevents the assertion of facts, then inquiry can never come to an end. Either Dewey neglected to include a way for symbolized facts to be asserted, or he should have dropped the strange notion that symbols prevent the assertion of those facts.

The next sentence reads, "The carrying on of inquiry requires that the facts be taken as *re*presentative and not just as *pre*-sented."[43] How can a fact be representative? Presumably it is representative if it represents something. Dewey, however, says nothing about facts which represent something. Facts could, of course, be used to represent things. They would then be what he, on page fifty-one of his *Logic*, calls either "signs" or "symbols", depending on whether or not they have a natural connection with what they represent. Here, however, Dewey is not talking about facts as being either of these. To answer the question how a fact can be representative, he says, "This demand is met by formulating them in propositions – that is, by means of symbols." [44] Something has been turned around here. It is the symbols that do the representing, not the facts. Hence it is the symbols which should be called "representative". That which is represented by the symbols ought not be called "representative".

There is, however, also the possibility that when Dewey says inquiry requires that facts be taken as "*re*presentative", he means the facts must be taken as presented again. This interpretation is open to two objections. First, this would be a misuse of "representative". Italicizing the first syllable does not change the meaning of the word. Secondly, the facts are not literally presented again when they are referred to in language any more than one literally sees ideas when they are referred to in language.

When Dewey says, as he did in the last passage quoted, that the demand that facts be representative is met by formulating them in propositions, he seems to imply that in all cases of inquiry the facts which play a part in the inquiry must be propositionally formulated. Now, of course, facts do play a part in every inquiry. Therefore, Dewey is, in effect, insisting that all inquiries are conducted using propositions. If Dewey is redefining "inquiry" so that this is true, then one can object that this is unwarranted stipulation. On the other hand, if Dewey is not redefining "inquiry", then he is quite wrong in holding that all inquiry is conducted with propositions. The grand experiments of science undoubtedly have used propositions, but frequently not the common, everyday inquiries of hunting for one's keys or finding the right road on a road map.

During the examination of Dewey's remarks on ideas, it was noted that he emphasized the operational character of ideas. That is, he stressed what ideas do, what they can be used for, what their function is, even to the point of defining them in these terms. In like manner Dewey emphasizes the operational character of facts, and, just as in the case of ideas, carrying the cause of operational-

---

[44] Dewey, *Logic*, p. 114.

ism to its furthest extremes has some odd results. "What is meant by calling facts operational? Upon the negative side what is meant is that they are not self-sufficient and complete in themselves." [45]

As Dewey has often done before, he begins a subject with a striking statement intended, it seems, to run counter to customary ways of thinking. If one were to read only this passage, one would think that Dewey must believe that all facts are somehow dependent on something else in order to exist, that, for example, the fact that the streets are icy is dependent on something else. The sentence following the one quoted above, however, places the matter in a rather different light. Dewey writes, "They are selected and described, as we have seen, for a purpose, namely statement of the problem involved in such a way that its material both indicates a meaning relevant to resolution of the difficulty and serves to test its worth and validity." [46] The meaning now seems to be that facts are neither self-sufficient nor complete only in the sense that they are selected and described for a purpose. This rather arbitrary reading of the phrase, "not self-sufficient and complete", renders the remark in which it is found much less interesting than it at first appeared, for it is hardly informative to say that the facts of an inquiry are picked for a purpose.

A few lines farther appears a related statement: "If 'the facts of the case' were final and complete in themselves, if they did not have a special operative force in resolution of the problematic situation, they could not serve as evidence." [47] The statement is written as if it were an argument for the contention that facts of the case are not final and complete in themselves. What is said, however, is a disguised tautology, first because by facts being "final and complete" Dewey means that they are such as serve to indicate solutions and act as evidence for them; and secondly, because the "special operative force" of facts refers, among other things, to their serving as evidence.

In one of the earlier quotations Dewey said that facts both suggest hypotheses and also test them. This is surely a sound

[45]   Dewey, *Logic*, p. 113.
[46]   Dewey, *Logic*, p. 113.
[47]   Dewey, *Logic*, p. 113.

observation. However, even here Dewey sows a few tares with the wheat, for he appears to hold that the same set of facts can do both, that the same set of facts can both suggest a hypothesis and test it. "They are selected and described, as we have seen, for a purpose, namely statement of the problem involved in such a way that its material both indicates a meaning relevant to resolution of the difficulty and serves to test its worth and validity." [48] Of course, one may conduct his inquiry this way if he wishes, but it certainly is not a method likely to reach a sound conclusion. It is not a good method because the hypothesis is not really tested unless it is compared with facts which are different from the facts which prompted the hypothesis. Suppose that one's automobile stalls, and will not start. Since the gauge shows that the gasoline is low, it is hypothesized that the motor will not start because the tank is empty. Dewey would have it, if our reading of him is correct, that the low reading on the gauge also serves to check the hypothesis. Of course, the motor may not start for any of a considerable number of reasons, any of which might coincide with a low gauge reading. Since the low gauge reading prompted the hypothesis, it surely cannot test it. Were this not the case, all hypotheses based on any observations at all would be tested hypotheses.

Elsewhere Dewey, himself, seems to be of this opinion. Speaking of the predicate of judgment, which is the same as what he earlier called an "idea", he writes, "The anticipation functions logically to instigate and direct an operation of experimental observation. When the consequences of the latter combine with facts already ascertained so as to constitute a unified total situation, inquiry comes to an end." [49] The "facts already ascertained" would, apparently, be the facts observed before the hypothesis (which he above calls "anticipation") is acted upon. The "consequences of the latter" would, presumably, be facts which are consequences of "experimental observation". Because these two sets of facts are said to "combine . . . so as to constitute a unified total situation" they must be distinct and different sets

[48] Dewey, *Logic*, p. 113.
[49] Dewey, *Logic*, p. 131.

of facts. The phrase, "to constitute a unified situation", refers, of course, to the hypothesis' being confirmed. Since Dewey holds that the hypothesis is confirmed by the two sets of facts combining, it is clear that he must also hold that the set which suggests the hypothesis cannot by itself confirm it.

III

JUDGMENT

After discussing Dewey's treatment of how a problem is developed and solved, it is appropriate to turn to what he has to say about the solution. The passages included here carry the burden of what Dewey says about the structure of that solution.

A. JUDGMENT AND PROPOSITIONS

Dewey's term for the solution to inquiry is "judgment". He writes, "In terms of the ideas set forth in the last chapter, judgment may be identified as the settled outcome of inquiry." [1] In limiting judgment to the solution or the settled outcome of inquiry, it is understood that Dewey is exercising his right to develop certain terms as technical terms within his system. He might have said that the settled outcome of inquiry is to be called a "pronouncement". He did, in fact, elsewhere call it a "grounded assertion" and a "warranted assertion". There can be no controversy here.

Upon reading further, however, it becomes evident that Dewey is setting up a concept of judgment which does not agree with the common notion of a solution to a problem. "It is concerned with the concluding objects that emerge from inquiry in their status of being conclusive. Judgment in this sense is distinguished from *propositions*. The content of the latter is intermediate and representative and is carried by symbols; while judgment, as finally made, has *direct* existential import." [2]

[1] John Dewey, *Logic: The Theory of Inquiry* (New York, 1938), p. 120.
[2] Dewey, *Logic*, p. 120.

Dewey contrasts judgments with propositions and bases this contrast on three properties of propositions: being intermediate, being representative, and being carried by symbols. By implication, this means that a judgment is none of these. About the first, there is no need to comment. Since judgment is the termination of inquiry, it is appropriate to say that it is not intermediate. By "representative" Dewey, presumably, means about the same as "being carried by symbols". That is, he seems to mean that something is representative in virtue of being carried by symbols. He has already made clear that a proposition is composed of symbols: "This process, operating with symbols (constituting propositions) . . ." [3] The implication of contrasting propositions with judgments on the basis of symbols is that a judgment is not composed of symbols. This is a rather surprising view. Does Dewey hold this view unambiguously?

Dewey illustrates the kind of judgment he has in mind with the example of a court trial. Regarding the sentence handed down by the judge, he says, "The final judgment arrived at is a settlement. The case is disposed of; the disposition takes effect in existential consequences . . . It is this resulting state of actual affairs – this changed situation – that is the matter of the final settlement or judgment." [4] Elsewhere in the volume he maintains the same point of view. "This emphasis upon requalification of antecedent existential material, and upon judgment as the resulting transformation, stands in sharp contrast with traditional theory." [5] ". . . judgment is a process of temporal existential reconstitution." [6] There are numerous other passages in which Dewey emphatically expresses the doctrine that judgment is the end product in a guided transformation of existing things. These all tend to strengthen the impression that judgment is not a sentence or a proposition.

There are, however, also passages which blur the distinction between a judgment and a proposition. Speaking again of the

[3] Dewey, *Logic*, p. 111.
[4] Dewey, *Logic*, pp. 121-122.
[5] Dewey, *Logic*, p. 159.
[6] Dewey, *Logic*, p. 133.

sentencing in a courtroom, Dewey says, "The sentence or proposition is not an end in itself but a decisive directive of future activities. The consequences of these activities bring about an existential determination of the prior situation which was indeterminate as to its issue." [7] There is a confusing choice of words in the first line. The context, however, makes it reasonably clear that the first four words mean something like, "The sentence which the judge hands down, which is a proposition . . ."

A neighboring passage reads, "The sentence itself is a proposition, differing, however, from the propositions formed during the trial, whether they concern matters of fact or legal conceptions, in that it takes overt effect in operations which construct a new qualitative situation." [8] It should perhaps be pointed out again that by "sentence" in this context Dewey does not mean a grammatical unit, nor does he mean judgment. It is the sentence which the judge hands down. The judgment is still the "existential transformation". The point of these two passages, however, is that they reveal a close connection between the sentence the judge hands down, which, we must remember, is also a proposition, and what Dewey calls "judgment". Although a judgment is not a proposition, it is related to one in that it is the performance of that which the proposition states. The judgment is the sentence carried out.

So far we have located passages which draw a sharp distinction between a proposition and a judgment, and passages which, while they in no wise remove that distinction, appear to soften it somewhat. In addition to these, however, there are also passages which clearly indicate that judgments are propositions. These are the passages which speak of the end of inquiry as being "warranted assertion" or "warranted assertibility".

If inquiry begins in doubt, it terminates in the institution of conditions which remove need for doubt. The latter state of affairs may be designated by the words *belief* and *knowledge*. For reasons that I shall state later I prefer the words "warranted assertibility". [9]

[7] Dewey, *Logic*, p. 121.
[8] Dewey, *Logic*, p. 122.
[9] Dewey, *Logic*, p. 7.

Knowledge in its strictest and most honorific sense is identical with
warranted assertion.[10]

It would be rather preposterous to say that Dewey means to have
two terminations of inquiry. That which is here called "warranted assertion" must, therefore, be the same as judgment. A judgment must be a warranted assertion. Since an assertion is a proposition, a judgment must also be a proposition. This, however, is
precisely what some of the passages previously quoted denied.

There is another argument which ends the same way, but which
begins a little differently. In the last chapter we learned that the
idea or hypothesis is stated as a proposition. After different
hypotheses are proposed, rejected, altered, and proposed again,
being constantly checked by the facts, the understanding surely
was that finally one of them would be supported by the facts. In
that case what previously had been a hypothetical proposition
now was a grounded and warranted proposition. This means that
the only difference between a hypothesis and a warranted proposition is not that one is a proposition and the other not, but that
one is a proposition supported by evidence while the other is a
proposition unsupported by evidence. Since a judgment is the
termination of inquiry and the termination of inquiry is a warranted proposition and a warranted proposition is, of course, a
proposition, a judgment is a proposition.

Furthermore, in the chapter from which most of the quotations
are now being selected, the chapter entitled "The Construction
of Judgment", Dewey has organized the material into several
sections. Three of these sections are entitled, "The Subject of
Judgment", "The Predicate of Judgment", and "The Copula".
It would, however, make no sense to talk about the subject,
predicate, and the copula of judgment if there were no subject,
predicate, or copula in judgment; and outside of language, which
in this context means especially propositions, there are none.

There seem, then, to be two distinct views which Dewey has
concerning the conclusion of inquiry. The one is that it is the end
state of the transformation of existing things, i.e., things which

10   Dewey, *Logic*, p. 143.

are not symbols. This view is in harmony with the definition of inquiry studied earlier in which it was said that the end of inquiry is a determinate situation and a unified whole. The other view is that the end of inquiry is a statement expressed in symbols and that this statement is supported by evidence.

Although Dewey is clearly inconsistent, it can, perhaps, be shown that it was quite natural to adopt both views and that, indeed, there is some truth in each of them.

Solutions to problems can, no doubt, be classified in various ways. A classification useful for our purposes and one which seems to be exhaustive is as follows: knowing how to do something, doing it, and knowing that something is the case. Which kind is appropriate depends both on the problem and how it is formulated. Consider the hunter lost in the woods. When is his problem solved? Is it solved when he reaches home or when he discovers how to get home? His problem was given as being lost; therefore, his problem is solved as soon as he is no longer lost. It would seem to be more accurate, then, to say that his problem is solved as soon as he discovers how to get home rather than to say that it is solved only when he actually reaches home. This is an example of a solution which is a knowing how to do something.

However, in this particular problem, that of being lost, the solution might also have been stated as, e.g., knowing that the path by the fallen oak is the correct path. This would be an example of knowing that something is the case. In this problem (but not necessarily in others) knowing how and knowing that have the same results. Each is a solution to the same problem, and, depending on more context than has so far been given, they may or may not be considered the same solution. If knowing how to find the way home involves only knowing that the path by the fallen oak is the correct path, the two solutions might be considered the same. If, however, there are other ways of reaching home, then knowing how to get home and knowing that the path by the oak is the correct path would, of course, be considered different solutions.

In general we can say that if the context is such that knowing how can be narrowed down to one or two or a very few directions, then knowing how can be restated as a knowing that. For example, knowing how to win a particular chess game may depend on knowing only one move. If one notices this move, he wins; if not, he loses. Since the problem is winning the game, the solution can be thought of as knowing how to make the next move; but it can also be thought of as knowing that such and such is the correct move. However, if the problem is learning to skate, knowing how is different from knowing that, for knowing that will only furnish one with directions, but knowing how involves knowing a skill.

Both of these solutions should be thought of as different from the third. The two mentioned are kinds of knowledge; the third is not. Imagine the hunter again, and this time let us reformulate the problem. His problem is not to discover the way home, but *to reach* home. Perhaps a storm is rising. In this case the problem is not solved until the hunter is actually home. The solution is not a case of knowledge, but of "existential transformation".

In all cases of knowing that and in those cases of knowing how which do not involve knowing a skill, the solution has a very close relation to language. When the solution is an existential transformation, this is not so. This difference can be expressed in three related, but somewhat varied ways. First, that kind of solution which is an item of knowledge (excluding skills) can be said to be achieved in virtue of establishing a certain proposition as true. The lost hunter has achieved the solution as soon as he has established, through recognition of a certain feature of the landscape, through memory, or whatever, that the proposition, "The path by the fallen oak is the correct one", is true. A starving man, however, has not solved his problem simply because he knows a certain proposition to be true. Secondly, a solution in the sense of knowledge (except for those which are skills) may be identified with a certain proposition. Such a proposition is called the "correct proposition" or the "answer". (Of course, not all answers are propositions.) On the other hand, a solution in the sense of a change in the world, an existential transformation, can surely not be identified with a proposition. There is no correct proposition which satisfies the starving man. Finally, a solution in the sense of knowledge (excepting skills) can be said to be expressed in a proposition. The proposition, "The path by the fallen oak is the correct one", expresses the solution to the problem. The solution is put into words. In the case of the existential kind of solution, however, the solution can be described and talked about, but not expressed. One does not express an existential arrangement, e.g., a landscape, one describes it. When the solution to a problem is knowledge (excluding skills), it is, like thoughts, not described, but expressed. In the examples above and perhaps in most cases, the relation between language and that which is expressed is more intimate than the relation between language and that which is described.

Dewey seems not to have noticed the different kinds of solutions to problems, and, since he has not noticed this difference, he also has not noticed that language is more closely associated with one than with the other. He, therefore, sometimes speaks of the solution as an existential, determinate, and unified situation, while at other times he speaks of it as a warranted and grounded assertion.

B. THE SUBJECT OF JUDGMENT

Dewey now addresses himself to the problem of the structure of judgment. The constituent parts of judgment are, he says, the subject, predicate, and copula. One thinks immediately that Dewey must have in mind judgment as being a warranted assertion, for the parts of judgment have the same nomenclature as the parts of a sentence. It comes, therefore, as a surprise to learn that the subject of judgment is made up of the facts of the case. "Observed facts of the case in their dual function of bringing the problem to light and of providing evidential material with respect to its solution constitute what has traditionally been called the *subject*." [11] The passage seems to say that all the observed facts constitute the subject. If this is what Dewey means, then it is, of course, incorrect if for no other reason than that all the facts of the case would make a rather unwieldy subject. Adopting Dewey's court-

[11] Dewey, *Logic*, p. 124.

room setting, in the judgment, "Tom is guilty", the subject is Tom. Presumably, in the course of the trial there are legal instruction, testimony, perhaps even exhibits. The facts of the case are made up of all of these. If the facts of the case constitute the subject, then they all should be judged guilty. This would, of course, be nonsense, for it is only Tom who is judged guilty.

There is, moreover, another reason why the facts of the case cannot be the subject of judgment. The subject of a proposition, at least usually, does not refer to a fact at all. "Tom" does not refer to a fact. An example of a proposition using a fact for a subject would be, "That Tom is guilty is the verdict of the court." Occasionally a proposition has a fact for a subject, but generally this is not so. Therefore, a general statement to the effect that facts constitute the subject is incorrect.

Dewey is, moreover, inconsistent, for he also says, "The subject is existential, either a singular *this*, or a set of singulars." [12] Singulars, however, are not facts. Tom is a singular, but not a fact. A fact is a state of affairs, not an object. It is expressed in several words, usually in a complete sentence, never in a single word. Yet, Dewey has previously said that the facts of the case constitute the subject, whereas in the above view he says that singulars do. The latter is, of course, the more reasonable view.

Although Dewey should not have said that the subject is made up of the facts of the case, there is a plausible explanation of why he did so. The key is the term, "subject matter". He uses that term in the familiar way in which it means roughly the matter or material of something. Thus, on one occasion he says, "One kind of operations deals with ideational or conceptual subject-matter. This subject-matter stands for possible ways and ends of resolution." [13] "Conceptual subject-matter" might be thought of as conceptual material, conceptual matter, or, more simply, just concepts. On another occasion he writes, "The subject-matter and methods of modern science have no such direct affinity with those of common sense as existed when classic science and logic were formulated." [14] In the first part the subject matter of modern science is contrasted with the methods of modern science. Here the subject matter might be thought of as that which modern science is about, that with which it is concerned, or, simply, the material of modern science.

In the following passage Dewey uses the term, "subject matter", in a way more like that with which we are concerned: "The copula in a judgment, in distinction from the term of formal relation, expresses, accordingly, the actual transformation of the subject-matter of an indeterminate situation into a determinate one." [15] Let us disregard the sentence as a whole and note only that Dewey speaks of the "transformation of the subject-matter of an indeterminate situation into a determinate one". Now one could perhaps say that there are two different subject matters, one at the beginning of inquiry, called "indeterminate subject matter", and one at the end, called "determinate subject matter". While one may, of course, look at Dewey's remarks in this way, there is no need to do so. In fact, a more natural reading is to say that there is only one subject matter. It is indeterminate at the beginning of inquiry, and at the end this same subject matter is determinate. If there is only one subject matter, it is more fitting to speak of "transformation", as Dewey does, whereas if there were two, it would be more fitting to use the terms, "exchange" or "substitution".

Among the several expressions which Dewey uses to refer to the conclusion of inquiry are both "judgment" and "determinate situation". A judgment and a determinate situation are, therefore, one and the same. Since they are one and the same, they must have the same subject matter. We have already said that the subject matter of the determinate situation is the same as the subject matter of the indeterminate situation, and we know from earlier material that the subject matter of the indeterminate situation is the facts of the case. Therefore, the subject matter of the determinate situation is also the facts of the case, and this, in turn, means that the subject matter of judgment is the facts of the

---

[14] Dewey, *Logic*, p. 97.
[15] Dewey, *Logic*, p. 135.

case. The question we are trying to answer is, "Why might Dewey have held the incorrect view that the subject of judgment is the facts of the case?" The answer which our line of reasoning suggests is that Dewey does not bother to distinguish between "subject" and "subject matter", that he goes from the correct view that the subject matter of judgment is the facts of the case to the incorrect view that the subject of judgment is the facts of the case.

Saying that the facts of the case constitute the subject of judgment is based on three mistakes: (1) Describing solution in general as a unified situation and a determinate subject matter. (Only that type of solution which is not a form of knowledge, but is rather a certain change in the world, should be so regarded.) (2) Describing solution in general as having a subject. (Only that type of solution which can be identified with a proposition, i.e., which excludes skills and existential transformation, should be so regarded.) (3) Confounding "subject matter" with "subject".

C.   OBJECTS

Within the treatment of judgment Dewey devotes considerable effort to a rather unusual view of objects and events. His discussion is really not as relevant here as it would have been earlier, either in his remarks on what a situation is, which we reviewed in the first chapter; or in his remarks on the place of facts in inquiry, which we reviewed in the second chapter. However, since Dewey does place his discussion of objects and events here and since the discussion does form a part of his doctrine of the subject of judgment, it is, perhaps, best left where it is.

This doctrine of objects is, apparently, of considerable importance to Dewey, as, indeed, it should be to any philosopher, for he edges into it no less than three times in the space of the chapter. Each time Dewey makes the transition into the matter in a different way. The doctrine is introduced on page 122. The transition is accomplished by saying that the subject matter of final judgment is a situation, then bringing in objects as a contrast to a situation. The second transition, found on page 125, is made by means of an argument against the view that an object or a quality is given to judgment. Dewey argues that an object or quality is subsequent, not prior to inquiry. On page 130 Dewey makes the third transition by reviewing Aristotle's doctrine of subject and substance, offering his own view of substance in contrast to that of Aristotle's – objects, in a broad sense, being the same as substance.

In order to follow Dewey more easily, it is, perhaps, better not to follow each of his three sorties because the same thoughts tend to turn up in each. Instead, items will be selected from each in such a way as to present a reasonable degree of progression without repetition.

The first matter to settle concerns the range of Dewey's doctrine of objects. What is included under "objects"? "The difference between a singular and an individual is the same as that previously pointed out between *an* object (or set of objects in their severalty) and a situation." [16] From this much we know that an object is contrasted with a situation. This is, of course, familiar from our earlier examination of Dewey's concepts of the situation.

"Singular objects exist and singular events occur within a field or situation." [17] This passage provides a comment on the relation between a singular and a situation. However, it is more important for this stage of the discussion to note that Dewey implies not only that objects are to be considered singulars, but that events are also.

"The given in the sense of the singular, whether object or quality . . ." [18] "This latter view holds that the existential matter, which has ultimately the form of *this object* or *this quality* . . ." [19] In these two passages the concept of the singular is broadened to include also qualities. A singular, then, may be an object, an event, or a quality. Dewey, however, does not usually list all three. Sometimes he uses the more general term, "singular". At

[16] Dewey, *Logic*, p. 123.
[17] Dewey, *Logic*, p. 123.
[18] Dewey, *Logic*, p. 124.
[19] Dewey, *Logic*, p. 125.

other times he refers to all three with the one word, "object", or with both "object" and "event". One could, perhaps, insist that when he says that an object has a certain characteristic, he is intentionally excluding events and qualities; that when he says that an event has a particular origin, he means an object and a quality do not; and so on. Such a reading, however, would fantastically multiply the complexity of Dewey's doctrine of objects, and, furthermore, it would quite obviously be an inaccurate and perverse reading. Rather, when Dewey says, as he does in the first passage quoted in our discussion of objects, that an object is to be contrasted with a situation, he is to be taken as meaning that events and qualities are also.

The following passage extends the identification of terms:

> The given in the sense of the singular, whether object or quality, is the special aspect, phase or constituent of the existentially present situation that is selected to locate and identify its problematic features with reference to the inquiry then and there to be executed. In the strict sense, it is *taken* rather than given. This fact decides the logical status of *data*. They are not isolated, complete or self-sufficient. To be a datum is to have a special function in control of the subject-matter of inquiry. It embodies a fixation of the problem in a way which indicates a possible solution. It also helps to provide evidence which tests the solution that is hypothetically entertained.[20]

Although Dewey could have been more lucid, the first half of the passage seems to imply that another word for singulars is "data", for he begins by talking about singulars and ends by saying that this determines the logical status of data. In the second half the function of data is described. This description is precisely the same as that furnished earlier for the facts of the case. The passage as a whole, then, allows one to identify singulars (objects, events, and qualities) with data, and data with facts of the case.

The series of identifications is not yet complete. It was said earlier that the facts of the case constitute the subject of judgment. Since singulars are identified with these facts, one can also say that singulars constitute the subject of judgment. Dewey says as

20   Dewey, *Logic*, p. 124.

much himself: "The subject is existential, either a singular *this,* or a set of singulars." [21]

The next identification Dewey makes, this one implicitly, is that a singular is a substance. One reason for inferring that Dewey makes this identification is that his description of substances is the same as his description of objects. "The condition – and the sole condition that has to be satisfied in order that there may be substantiality, is that certain qualifications hang together as dependable signs that certain consequences will follow when certain interactions take place." [22] "An object, in other words, is a set of qualities treated as *potentialities* for specified existential consequences." [23] Another reason is that Dewey gives the same things as examples of both substances and objects, as when he says, "Sugar, for example, is a substance . . ." [24] and "The object, *sugar* . . ." [25] Finally, Dewey speaks of certain things being "substantial objects", indicating, it appears, that they are both substances and objects: ". . . water as a substantial object . . ." [26] "The greater the number of interactions, of operations, and of consequences, the more complex is the constitution of a given substantial object." [27] "They did not become *entirely* new substantial objects . . ." [28] "Being a substantial object . . ." [29] ". . . the functional nature of substantial objects." [30]

One might think that the word, "substance", means object in the narrow sense (a chair, a piece of granite), but not in the broad sense in which it means the same as "singular". This is not so. Dewey specifically extends the word, "substance", to include events, and presumably qualities are included also. "In the light of dependable inferences that can be drawn, of the correlations of changes that are established, an event like a flash of

[21] Dewey, *Logic*, p. 127.
[22] Dewey, *Logic*, pp. 128-129.
[23] Dewey, *Logic*, p. 129.
[24] Dewey, *Logic*, p. 128.
[25] Dewey, *Logic*, p. 128.
[26] Dewey, *Logic*, p. 129.
[27] Dewey, *Logic*, p. 129.
[28] Dewey, *Logic*, p. 129.
[29] Dewey, *Logic*, p. 129.
[30] Dewey, *Logic*, p. 130.

lightning has *logical* solidity and endurance in spite of its existential transitivity. It is substantial." [31]

No criticism is intended in the foregoing identification of terms, although one may well wonder if Dewey realized what he was saying. It comes as something of a relief, however, to learn that Dewey is not talking about so many different things as it at first appeared. It is helpful to have the vocabulary reduced to a more workable level.

In the first chapter when Dewey's concept of the situation was being examined, we took incidental notice of his treatment of objects and events. The following is a passage which was quoted there and which shows how he would have objects and events differ from a situation: "In actual experience, there is never any such isolated singular object or event; *an* object or event is always a special part, phase, or aspect, of an environing experienced world – a situation." [32] It will, perhaps, be recalled from our examination of Dewey's concept of the situation that a possible, though not altogether certain, interpretation of the passage was that an object or event does not exist except as a part of an experienced situation. Another and less novel interpretation was that objects may exist independently of any experienced situation, but that they cannot be perceived independently. After reading Dewey's more extended remarks on the subject, does one interpretation appear more strongly supported than the other?

Let us try to assemble first those statements which support the latter and less controversial view that objects may exist independently of any experienced situation, but that they cannot be perceived independently.

The discriminative or differential aspect of the demonstrative act and its singular object is suggested in ordinary speech by the expression "pointing *out*". It is impossible merely to point *at* something. For anything or everything in the line of vision or gesture may be equally pointed *at*. The act of pointing is wholly indeterminate as to its object. It is not selective within a situation, because it is not controlled by the problem which the situation sets . . .[33]

[31]   Dewey, *Logic*, p. 130.
[32]   Dewey, *Logic*, p. 67.
[33]   Dewey, *Logic*, p. 124.

It can hardly be correct to say both that pointing is wholly indeterminate and that anything in the line of vision or gesture may be pointed at. Surely if what is pointed at is limited to the line of vision, pointing is not "wholly indeterminate". In spite of this inaccuracy, the basic idea is clear. The significance of the passage with respect to a doctrine of objects is that the passage as a whole is about distinguishing an object and that it is not about the existence of that object. The notion that successful pointing requires a problem for context seems to refer to perception only and is surely quite compatible with the rather different notion that the object may exist apart from the pointing and the problem.

Another passage which supports the position that Dewey holds merely that it is the perception of objects rather than their existence which depends on an experienced situation, reads, "There is, however, no incompatibility between the fact that *it* is just what it existentially is and the estimate that it is the needed evidential ground of a definite characterization." [34] Speaking of an object's being what it existentially is would seem to refer to the existence of an object together with its several properties. However, "the estimate that it is the needed evidential ground of a definite characterization" refers to the role of objects in inquiry. The passage says, in effect, that there is no incompatibility between the existence of an object together with certain properties, and its utilization in inquiry. If one makes a point of saying that two things are not incompatible, it must be understood that they are at least separable. Thus, this passage suggests that an object may exist even though it has no role in inquiry.

Although this passage by itself seems clear, Dewey proceeds to give an explanation of it which serves only to perplex. "Stating the matter positively, the operations that institute a 'this' as subject are always selective-restrictive of something from out of a larger field." [35] This explanation certainly is not merely a positive rendering of the passage previously quoted. It expresses a different thought altogether. It can, in fact, be taken as the first of those passages which provide evidence for adopting the more

---

[34] Dewey, *Logic*, p. 127.
[35] Dewey, *Logic*, p. 127.

radical interpretation of Dewey's doctrine of objects, namely, the interpretation which says the very existence of an object depends on its being a part of an experienced situation.

A second passage, carrying a similar message reads, "Singular objects exist and singular events occur within a field or situation." [36] This sentence can be understood according to either interpretation; however, let us note that Dewey says "singular objects exist" in such a way and "singular events occur" in such a way. This appears to mean that they do not exist or occur in any other way. The passage would, therefore, be evidence for saying that objects do not exist and events do not occur apart from a situation.

Another passage reads, "*This* or *that* star, man, rock or whatever, is always a discrimination or selection made for a purpose, or for the sake of some objective consequence within an inclusive field." [37] Dewey might mean only that the discrimination is made for a purpose. On the other hand, it is more probable that he means that apart from such discrimination there simply is no object. If he had meant the former, he would not have said, "This ... star ... is always a discrimination ..." It would have been clearer to have said, "The discrimination of this star is always made for a purpose ..."

"The singular is that upon which inquiry into an individual situation pivots under the special conditions that at a given time fix the problem with respect to the conditions to be dealt with forthwith." [38] Dewey says, "The singular is that upon which inquiry ... pivots ..." The most plausible reading of this is that Dewey means the singular is nothing else. If he had meant only that the singular may, on occasion, be used as that upon which inquiry pivots, he should have phrased it differently. Saying that the singular is so and so strongly suggests that it would not be a singular if it were not so and so.

Whereas the quotations so far have supported one view or the other simply by being opinions, the next two quotations are argu-

[36]   Dewey, *Logic*, p. 123.
[37]   Dewey, *Logic*, p. 123.
[38]   Dewey, *Logic*, pp. 123-124.

ments. "If its object is taken to be complete in itself, loss of differential force destroys all power of reference on the part of the demonstrative act. The very existence of differentiation, on the other hand, shows that the singular exists within an extensive field." [39] The first sentence implies that if an object can be differentiated, it is not complete in itself. Before this can be commented on or even understood, we must know what Dewey means when he talks about an object's being complete in itself. One meaning is that the object exists independently of anything else, that it requires nothing else in order to exist. This meaning would make the whole passage worthwhile. However, if this is the meaning, the consequence clause does not follow from the antecedent; that is, it does not follow that if an object can be referred to, it depends on something else for its existence. The supposed implication just is not there.

A second interpretation of what Dewey means by referring to an object as being complete in itself is that an object cannot be perceived outside of a context. If one adopts this interpretation, then what Dewey says is true because, interpreted, it means that if an object can be differentiated, it is perceived in a context. This, however, is also trivial because "being differentiated" means being differentiated from something else and this something else can be thought of as the context. The full statement would be that if an object can be differentiated from a context, then it is perceived in a context.

The second sentence is sufficiently similar to the first so that it does not need a separate discussion.

The second argument for the position that the very existence of objects depends on an experienced situation follows a somewhat different course. Let us look first at some preliminary material.

In this section, I shall consider the *subject* of judgment. The bearing of the conclusions reached up to this point may be focalized by contrasting them with a doctrine current in logical theory. This latter view holds that the existential matter, which has ultimately the form of *this object* or *this quality,* is given or presented in a literal sense *to* judgment. Judgment proper is then confined to the work of predi-

[39] Dewey, *Logic,* p. 123.

cating something of it, of characterizing what is handed out ready-made either to sense-perception or to judgment . . . The contrasting position here taken holds that the subject-matters of subject and predicate are determined in correspondence with each other in and by the process of "thought", that is, inquiry.[40]

The passage is about what should be considered the subject of judgment. This question is really the same as the question about the nature of the object, for, as Dewey sees it, if the object is literally given to judgment it exists independently and is not determined by judgment. If an object is not given to judgment, then it does not exist independently and is determined by that judgment. These things are mentioned in order to support the notion that what follows is as much about the nature of objects *per se* as it is about the nature of the subject of judgment.

The argument, itself, is as follows:

We begin by pointing out the difficulties, amounting to impossibilities, in the customary view advanced in many standard treatises. (1) It leaves judgment, as predication, and just at the point where its existential material is concerned, entirely at the mercy of the accidental flux of objects which happen to present themselves. It thereby destroys the possibility of sequential continuity in "thought". Predication would at one moment be characterizing one object, and at the next moment some other object, according as changes and shifts in environing conditions took place.[41]

According to Dewey unless one adopts the view that the existence of objects depends on inquiry, one is committed to the notion that judgment, indeed thought, itself, is impossible because the object is not around long enough. Since judging and thinking take time, one might begin a judgment about one thing and find himself finishing the judgment about something else because of "the accidental flux of objects which happen to present themselves". Of course, we realize that we can think and make judgments; so, it seems, objects must be dependent on inquiry.

The error of the argument is that Dewey has equivocated on the word, "object". The kind of object which is susceptible to accidental flux is an object of thought. (Furthermore, it is really

40 Dewey, *Logic*, p. 125.
41 Dewey, *Logic*, p. 125.

incorrect to call this flux "accidental", for purposes, needs, habits, and the familiar laws of the association of ideas affect it.) The kind of object which makes up a subject of judgment is generally not an object of thought. A judgment, for example, may be about a star. In such a case it is important to insist that it is about a star, not about the experience of seeing a star or the thought of a star. The star is an object, but not an object of thought, as Dewey is using that term. By referring to "the accidental flux of objects which happen to present themselves" and also to "the customary view" of the subject of judgment, Dewey refers to two entirely different meanings of "object". This allows him to develop what at first appears to be a strong argument for the view that the existence of an object depends on inquiry.

At the beginning of the examination of Dewey's view of objects, it was asked whether the conservative view (that objects may exist independently of any experienced situation, but that they are not perceived independently) or the radical view (that objects do not exist except as a part of an experienced situation) received stronger endorsement. It now seems reasonably safe to say that Dewey favors the radical view. We must remember, however, that passages have been advanced which support also the more conservative position. Apparently, then, Dewey holds both and, thus, is involved once again in inconsistency. Furthermore, the position that the existence of objects depends on an experienced situation is actually a form of idealism, a movement Dewey outspokenly depreciated. The other view, that the perception of objects depends on there being a context, is generally regarded as true, but it is not a view philosophers have been disposed to dispute.

A question closely related to how objects exist and are perceived is the question of how they are identified.

The nub of any existential identification or characterization of a thing as such-and-such lies in the ground it offers for giving the object a description in terms of what is *not* then and there observed.[42]

The condition – and the sole condition that has to be satisfied in order that there may be substantiality, is that certain qualifications

[42] Dewey, *Logic*, p. 126.

hang together as dependable signs that certain consequences will follow when certain interactions take place.[43]

We speak regularly of chemical substances. A chemical substance is represented not by enumeration of qualities as such, but by a formula which provides a synoptic indication of the various types of consequences which will result.[44]

The perceptible qualities of table sugar and sugar of lead are much the same. Even common sense learns to distinguish them as different "substances" in virtue of some of the different consequences which ensue from their operational use.[45]

No explanation seems needed as to what Dewey means. The passages pertain to how objects are identified. There can be no disagreement with the view that identification is often performed in part on the basis of qualities which are revealed only after some operation has been performed on the object, and that in some cases, for example, the more subtle objects of recent science, the identification is performed wholly in this way. Dewey, however, goes beyond this to say that all identification is performed in a way that relies on operations. He states firmly that identification is not made on the basis of qualities present at the time the identification is made, that it is made only on the basis of qualities which are the result of operations.

When sitting down to work, one discriminates a pen from the other objects on his desk not by first doing something to it and waiting to see what will happen, but wholly on the basis of its color, shape, and size. In the last passage quoted Dewey gives an example of identifying on the basis of consequences. He seems to use the fact that sugar cannot be distinguished from sugar of lead on the basis of color as a reason for saying that color is not used at all in any identification. This is manifestly incorrect. Even if the color does not distinguish sugar from sugar of lead, it does distinguish each from a great many other things. Usually several different qualities are used to identify something, and, even though one of the several may not do the job alone, it is not

[43] Dewey, *Logic*, pp. 128-129.
[44] Dewey, *Logic*, p. 129.
[45] Dewey, *Logic*, pp. 129-130.

for that reason to be regarded as playing no part in identification. The first objection, therefore, to this doctrine of identification is that when measured against examples it is demonstrably false.

In order to understand Dewey's position on identification, we need to know more precisely what an operation is. The red color of a traffic light would, presumably, be a safe example of a quality immediately present. However, if the day were foggy and one had to drive closer and had to peer at the light intently in order to see it, would it still be an immediate quality, or would it be the result of an operation? Suppose that one vaguely hears a sound but cannot identify it unless he rolls down the window. Is rolling down the window an operation? Perhaps he still cannot identify the sound unless he also pays close attention. Is paying attention an operation? If paying attention is considered an operation, is it also an operation if one pays attention from the start? We must, of course, be alert to the fallacy of the beard and not conclude that there are no real operations because there is no distinct boundary between what is an operation and what is not. However, because Dewey is presenting a new and controversial doctrine of identification and because this doctrine rests on the concept of operation, it is important that the vagueness, harmless though it may be in other contexts, be reduced in this one. There is too much that is left unsaid when Dewey says that objects are identified on the basis of consequences to operations.

Perhaps a fairly accurate understanding of what led Dewey to his position can be achieved by means of another example. Consider the geologist hunting for a certain rock specimen. If he has to dig to find it, digging would, presumably, be considered an operation. Suppose, however, that he finds the rock by accident as he passes by on an errand. It would now seem incorrect to say that he identified the rock by means of qualities which were the result of operations. Dewey, by thinking only of cases like the former in which the geologist must dig, or the chemist must add a reagent, or the biologist must use a microscope, fails to allow for the many more cases in which objects are identified without anything resembling what we ordinarily call "operations".

In the examples Dewey furnishes he appears to shift his account somewhat. While he has described identification as depending on qualities which are the result of operations, he, in his examples, makes identification depend on the use of the object.

When it was discovered that wood-pulp could be used for making paper if its material was subjected to operations in which it entered into new conditions of interaction, the *significance* of certain forms of lumber as objects changed. They did not become *entirely* new substantial objects because old potentialities for consequences remained. But neither was it the same old substance.[46]

Powder is what will explode under certain conditions; water as a substantial object is that group of connected qualities which will quench thirst, and so on.[47]

To common sense, water is that which is pot*able*, which will cleanse, upon which many things will float, etc.[48]

These characteristic uses can, of course, be thought of as qualities. It can be thought of as a quality of a thing that it can be used in such and such a way. Nevertheless, it alters one's way of thinking about objects and suggests that underlying his varied remarks, Dewey is urging a strictly functional view of objects – that an object is what it is, not because of how it looks or tastes or feels; not because if you boil it, it will vaporize and disappear, or if you cool it, it will become hard and brittle; but because it quenches thirst and puts out fires.

A purely functional view of objects is, however, factually incorrect. We do not as a matter of fact view objects this way. Water may be understood as something which quenches thirst and puts out fires; but it is also a part of the concept that it is a colorless, tasteless liquid, and being a colorless, tasteless liquid is not one of the uses of water. To reuse an old example to illustrate a different principle, a hammer is not only something used to drive and pound things, but is also something having a head fixed crosswise to a handle. It has been acknowledged earlier in respect to definitions and, therefore, should be no more than mentioned now in respect to identifications, that function is an important feature.

[46]   Dewey, *Logic*, p. 129.
[47]   Dewey, *Logic*, p. 129.
[48]   Dewey, *Logic*, p. 130.

Indeed, in some definitions and identifications function carries the entire load. However, it is simply incorrect to say that it always does. The identification of something as water or of something else as a hammer relies on appearance and structure as well as use. Other identifications are based on the source of a thing, still others on what kinds of things accompany it, and so on. Dewey is right, of course, in pointing out Aristotle's error in supposing that there is a rigid, clear-cut distinction between what is a defining property and what is not; but he is wrong in supposing that all defining properties are the uses of a thing.

D. THE PREDICATE

Let us now leave Dewey's doctrine of objects and with it, his account of the subject of judgment. The other two parts of judgment, the predicate and the copula, receive considerably less attention. Concerning the predicate, Dewey writes,

The meanings which are suggested as possible solutions of a problem, which are then used to direct further operations of experimental observation, form the predicational content of judgments. The latter is related to the factual content, that is, the subject, as the possible to the actual . . . It possesses *logical* status only as it is taken for what it is *qua* predicate – namely, a *method* of solution not itself a solution.[49]

Dewey here lists three functions of the predicate: it suggests solutions, it directs new observations, and it is a method of solution. Presumably it is the second and third in virtue of being the first; that is, it directs new observation and is a method of solution in virtue of being a suggested solution.

In any case, one is reminded of Dewey's description of ideas. "The possible solution presents itself, therefore, as an *idea* . . ." [50] "Ideas are operational in that they instigate and direct further operations of observation; they are proposals and plans for acting upon existing conditions to bring new facts to light and to organ-

---

[49] Dewey, *Logic*, p. 131.
[50] Dewey, *Logic*, p. 109.

ize all the selected facts into a coherent whole." [51] There appears
to be confusion here. The description of the predicate of judgment
doubtlessly fits ideas as well. This means that one can say that
ideas constitute the predicate of judgment. The ideas, however,
were said to be hypotheses, and hypotheses are complete propositions. "The conceptual and 'rational' contents are *hypotheses*." [52]
If it requires a whole proposition to express an idea, how can
just the predicate of judgment do it? Perhaps with an effort a
predicate can be put in propositional form, but the result is hardly
a judgment. The predicate must be a whole statement, persumably
in conditional form. If the predicate is a statement, then the subject must be something which can stand in some sort of relation
(expressed by the main verb) to that statement. An example
might be, "The judge said, 'If Tom confesses, he is guilty'."
Such a statement would never terminate a trial and would, therefore, not be a judgment. Presumably Dewey did not intend that
the predicate should be expressed by a proposition at all, but this
means only that he has not explained how a predicate can now
express what previously required a whole proposition to express.

In saying that the predicate of judgment suggests solutions to
problems, that it guides new operations, and that it is not the solution itself, but only a method of solution, Dewey appears to
forget what he has said a judgment is. Twelve pages earlier, in
beginning the chapter on judgment, he wrote, "In terms of the
ideas set forth in the last chapter, judgment may be identified as
the settled outcome of inquiry. It is concerned with the concluding
objects that emerge from inquiry in their status of being conclusive. Judgment in this sense is distinguished from *propositions*." [53]
Saying that judgment is "the settled outcome of inquiry" means
that judgment is the solution to the problem. If, however, it is the
solution, it is nonsense to continue to refer to "possible solutions
of a problem". Furthermore, if judgment is "the settled outcome
of inquiry", then neither are the other characteristics which
Dewey has applied to the predicate appropriate. There is no pos-

51 Dewey, *Logic*, pp. 112-113.
52 Dewey, *Logic*, p. 132.
53 Dewey, *Logic*, p. 120.

sible utility in further observations or in methods of solution if the solution is already achieved. Contrary to his definition of "judgment", Dewey, in discussing the predicate of judgment, appears to regard judgment as something very tentative. He seems to regard judgment, not at all as the termination of inquiry, but merely as a step toward that termination.

E. THE COPULA

The final section of Dewey's discussion of the structure of judgment has to do with the copula. Much of what he says leaves one with the feeling that he must choose between concluding that Dewey cannot mean what he seems to mean and that he is, therefore, extremely obscure, or that he does mean what he seems to mean and that he is quite incorrect, inconsistent, or both. He begins with the following: "It is neither a separate and independent element nor yet does it affect the predicate alone, attaching the latter to an independently and externally given singular subject, whether the latter be taken to be an object, a quality, or a sense-datum." [54] The copula, it is said, is not a separate and independent element. It affects both the predicate and the subject. Perhaps the thought can be explained in this way. Since "is" is the copula in the sentence, "Tom is guilty", it, in virtue of being a part of the sentence, can be said to be neither separate nor independent. Furthermore, since it appears between the words, "Tom" and "guilty", and since "Tom" and "guilty" do not express singly what they express when "is" appears between, the copula, "is", can be said to connect or attach the subject to the predicate. When we separate what the passage says about the subject of judgment from what it says about the copula, rephrase the remarks about the copula, and apply them to an example, it turns out that Dewey is merely saying that "is" is a part ("neither a separate and independent element") of the sentence, "Tom is guilty", and that "is" appears between "Tom" and

[54] Dewey, *Logic*, p. 132.

"guilty" to make a new language unit ("it affects both the predicate and the subject").

Dewey also says of the copula, "It does express the act of predication. But it also expresses the act or operation of 'subjection'; that is, of constituting the subject." [55] It is difficult to understand what an act of predication can be, unless it is simply applying a predicate to something, i.e., qualifying or describing something. In that case it is expressed, not by the copula, "is", but by the copula, the predicate, and the subject. It is expressed by the whole sentence. Ascribing guilt to Tom is not expressed by "is", but by "Tom is guilty". What the operation of subjection might be and how the copula can express the act of subjection is rather a mystery. It is not made any clearer by saying that the operation of subjection is constituting the subject.

Speaking again of the copula, Dewey writes,

It is a name for the complex of operations by means of which (a) certain existences are restrictively-selected to delimit a problem and provide evidential testing material, and by which (b) certain conceptual meanings, ideas, hypotheses, are used as characterizing predicates.[56]

The copula in a judgment, in distinction from the term of formal relation, expresses, accordingly, the actual transformation of the subject-matter of an indeterminate situation into a determinate one.[57]

These passages would serve much better as the description of the entire process of inquiry. If "is" is the name for the operations assigned above, it must mean the same as "inquiry". This is absurd. The little word, "is", certainly is not a synonym for "inquiry" and does not begin to refer to all the things Dewey lists. Furthermore, Dewey says, ". . . the copula stands for operations . . ." [58] and then in the explanation, describes the familiar process of reasoning. How it is that the copula can name all the processes which make up inquiry and can also stand only for, or especially for the process of reasoning, Dewey does not say.

[55] Dewey, *Logic*, p. 132.
[56] Dewey, *Logic*, p. 132-133.
[57] Dewey, *Logic*, p. 135.
[58] Dewey, *Logic*, p. 133.

IV

TRUTH

Dewey's theory of truth is closely related to his theory of inquiry. It is, therefore, helpful to be acquainted with his theory of inquiry before trying to understand his theory of truth. In discussing Dewey's theory of inquiry it seemed best to limit the discussion to the account found in his *Logic: The Theory of Inquiry* because this account is more detailed and recent than others. Furthermore, there seemed to be less danger that key words would have different meanings if they were written at one time than if they were written over a span of many years. One would like, in turning to Dewey's theory of truth, to limit oneself again to examining the account found in the *Logic*. However, although one might expect to find truth treated in a book on logic, it receives scant mention. The principal statement on truth, in fact, appears as only a footnote. In order to present Dewey's theory of truth, therefore, with any degree of adequacy, it is necessary to go beyond the *Logic* and to draw from several of his other books as well. This will, however, not be necessary until the latter part of the chapter.

A. DEFINITIONS OF "TRUTH" BORROWED FROM PEIRCE

Let us begin with the footnote appearing in the *Logic*. As Dewey, himself, acknowledges, it is really a statement by Peirce which Dewey is using.

The point of departure of the examination of this footnote is Bertrand Russell's criticisms of it and Dewey's rejoinder, both appearing in one volume.[1] The footnote, itself, reads as follows:

The best definition of *truth* from the logical standpoint which is
known to me is that of Peirce: "The opinion which is fated to be
ultimately agreed to by all who investigate is what we mean by the
truth, and the object represented by this opinion is the real." ... A
more complete (and more suggestive) statement is the following:
"Truth is that concordance of an abstract statement with the ideal
limit towards which endless investigation would tend to bring scientific belief, which concordance the abstract statement may possess by
virtue of the confession of its inaccuracy and one-sidedness, and this
confession is an essential ingredient of truth." [2]

The first definition begins, " 'The opinion which is fated to be
ultimately agreed to by all who investigate is what we mean by
the truth . . .' " The word, "truth", is sometimes used in this way,
as when one speaks of the "truth of science". Another and perhaps more common usage is to speak of truth as being a characteristic of an opinion. Certainly there are many other uses as well,
but the two above are perhaps the most common. These two ways
of using "truth" are so related that one can be explained in terms
of the other by saying that a truth is an opinion which is true.

The definition states that truth is the opinion which is fated to
be ultimately agreed to by all who investigate. It should be pointed out, not in the sense of criticism, but for clarification only,
that there is implied some phrase such as, "a given problem",
after the word, "investigate". Suppose that all who investigate
agree to the opinion that a two-party system is an asset to a
democracy, but one investigates the annual rainful of Nova
Scotia, another investigates the economic effects of high taxes, a
third the effect of solar explosions on the weather. Such investigations would, of course, be irrelevant to the question of whether a
two-party system is an asset to a democracy. Dewey undoubtedly
means that truth is the opinion which is fated to be ultimately
agreed to by all who investigate a given problem.

The definition says that truth is the opinion which will be ulti-

---

[1] *The Philosophy of John Dewey*, ed. Paul Arthur Schilpp (New York,
1951).
[2] John Dewey, *Logic: The Theory of Inquiry* (New York, 1938), p. 345.

mately agreed to ... and so on. (Let us drop the word, "fated", since no one supposes that Dewey is suggesting that there is a destiny shaping events.) It is important to note that the definition does not say that an opinion is not true until all who investigate agree to that opinion. This allows for the possibility of the opinion's being true before investigations are performed. Furthermore, the definition does not even require that an investigation be performed, for it speaks of the opinion which will be ultimately agreed to by *all who* investigate a certain problem. An opinion is false, not because no one investigates the problem, but because at least one who investigates it disagrees. According to the terms of the definition, therefore, an opinion may be true, not only if an investigation has not yet occurred, but also if one never occurs. The definition makes truth independent of there being an investigation, but very much dependent, if there is an investigation, on its having a certain result.

"Truth" is defined as being the opinion which will ultimately be agreed to by all who investigate a given problem. At first glance, this seems to mean that in order to determine whether or not an opinion is true one need check only those who have investigated the problem and inquire of them whether they agree with that opinion. Actually, however, one would be obliged to check everyone because one would first have to learn who had investigated the problem. "Everyone" includes also persons of both the past and the future. In those cases in which we know that it was impossible for a people in a certain locality or of a certain era to have investigated a given problem, the check is perhaps not necessary. For example, it would not seem necessary to check persons who lived long ago on whether they had investigated the nature of protons and neutrons. When one includes also the recent past, however, there are not many problems which those no longer alive might not have investigated. Since the investigations and opinions of most of the deceased are not recorded, checking these is usually impossible. This means, by the terms of the definition, that the truth of by far most opinions can never be known.

Furthermore, the poll must also include all who will live in the future. Just this requirement alone makes the checking impossible except for the last person alive. In virtue of the necessity of checking in both directions, the definition implies that it is impossible for us, at this time, to know whether any opinion is true or not, and that it is impossible for anyone to know whether any opinion is true or not except for the last survivor, and then only in respect to opinions that no person dead could have investigated.

Let us apply this definition to a couple of examples. Suppose the problem to be a scientific one, such as, "Does unconfined gas expand when heated?" The opinion being checked, let us say, is that unconfined gas does expand when heated. Is this opinion true or false? To find out one must check every person, those now dead, those who live now, and those who will live, to learn if each has investigated the properties of a gas when heated. Each person who has investigated this must be further questioned to learn whether he agrees with the opinion that unconfined gas expands when heated. Because we cannot check those who will live in the future, the truth at this time is incompletely tested; and because no one can check all those who lived in the past, no one will ever know whether it is true or not that unconfined gas expands when heated.

A second problem is not a scientific one. It is, "Is Tom's coat in the closet?" Tom's opinion is that it is. According to the definition, that opinion is not checked by going to the closet and looking. It is checked by polling the opinions of persons who have investigated the problem. Perhaps it is safe enough to omit checking the people of the past on this matter, but one presumably would have to check all present and future persons. The opinion is not thoroughly tested until the last man is counted, for it is always possible that he may investigate the problem and come up with an opinion that Tom's coat was not in the closet.

The observations so far are intended for clarification rather than for criticism. It is tempting to say that this definition of "truth" is incorrect because it makes it impossible to determine whether or not a given opinion is true except for the last survivor, and then only in respect to problems which those deceased could not have investigated. If this observation is to be a successful criticism, however, one must first successfully argue (and not merely venture the opinion) that we have the means for establishing whether or not an opinion is true. Likewise, it is tempting to say that the definition is wrong because it describes a method of testing which we do not use. In order for this observation to show the definition to be defective, one must first successfully argue that our methods of testing are the correct ones, and, indeed, the only correct ones.

Nevertheless, the definition clearly is wanting in several respects. One defect is that the method of determining truth implied by this definition is not the one Dewey wants. The method he wants is the method described in his account of inquiry, whereas the method the definition explicitly espouses is that of polling opinions.

Another and more serious objection comes to mind as soon as one imagines this method of verification adopted by everyone. A true opinion has been described as the one with which all who investigate the problem agree. The only way, then, that one can know whether his opinion is true or not is by checking the opinions of others. This method of checking opinions, however, must be the path to the knowledge of truth for others also. When one checks with a certain person to learn whether he has investigated the changes which occur when unconfined gas is heated, and it turns out that he has, this means only that this person has previously made a poll of his own. Again, if his poll reveals anyone who has made an investigation into the properties of unconfined gas being heated, this means only that that person has conducted a poll of his own. It is clear that we have nothing more than a collection of opinions based upon opinions, extending to infinity, and nowhere a person who has worked with gas.

A related criticism can be made from the other direction. When Dewey says that truth is the opinion which all who investigate will agree to, he doubtlessly has in mind conventional kinds of investigation involving the heating and measuring of a gas. The opinion that unconfined gas expands when heated is true if all *such* investigators agree to that opinion. The point is that the definition of "truth" on the one hand explicitly recognizes a certain method of verification, while on the other hand it is implicitly based upon a quite different method of verification. The former is verification by checking the opinions of those who have investigated a given problem; the latter is made up of all reputable scientific methods, especially those which Dewey explained in his theory of inquiry. In short, the definition explicitly espouses the view that verification comes by polling and implicitly espouses the view that verification comes by scientific procedure.

Even though a definition must be kept as short as possible, it is another defect of the definition that it lumps all investigators together. If one were trying to learn whether the opinion is true that unconfined gas expands when heated and proceeded to check the opinions of those who had investigated the problem, should he give all opinions equal weight? Since the definition says nothing to the contrary, presumably he should. Little imagination is required to see what folly this would be. Concerning celestial matters, the opinions of modern astronomers would count for no more than the opinions of ancient astrologers. The opinion of an Einstein would do no more to settle the truth about some matter in physics than the opinion of a boy with a Gilbert set.

There is yet another objection to this theory of truth. Suppose that, regarding an opinion, all who investigate agree save one. The definition requires that in order for there to be truth, agreement must be complete. Therefore, if one disagrees, the opinion is untrue. Our language is such that if a statement is untrue, its negation is usually true. (By saying "usually true" allowance is made for those cases in which a description is inaccurate, neither clearly right nor clearly wrong.) The definition before us, however, alters the very structure of the language in such a way that whenever a statement is untrue, its negation is also untrue.

Let us suppose that the opinion is that fireflies give off cold light. Many boys and few entomologists have, no doubt, investigated fireflies and have agreed with this opinion. Let us, however, suppose that one boy of somewhat heightened imagination believed that the insect felt warm. He had investigated fireflies and had arrived at an opinion. The fact that he disagreed with all the others is, according to the definition, sufficient to render the opinion untrue. If the uniformity of nature extends to fireflies and they are all alike in respect to how they produce light, we should be able to conclude that if it is not true that fireflies give off cold light, it must be true that they give off warm or incandescent light. According to Dewey's definition, however, this also is not true because there is likewise disagreement about the opinion that fireflies give off incandescent light.

Dewey's definition, therefore, has these implications: first, that the disagreement of one person can render an opinion untrue; secondly, that although an opinion is untrue, its negative is also untrue. The former renders the ordinary kinds of testing of opinions useless by giving unreasonable veto power to the individual. The latter upsets the very structure of our language in a way which, if the definition were adopted, would severely cripple communication.

The passage quoted at the beginning of this discussion contains also another definition. This second definition, still quoting Dewey's quotation from Peirce, reads, "Truth is that concordance of an abstract statement with the ideal limit towards which endless investigation would tend to bring scientific belief, which concordance the abstract statement may possess by virtue of the confession of its inaccuracy and one-sidedness, and this confession is an essential ingredient of truth." There is suggested in this definition the image of a geometrical asymptote. The curved line approaches the axis closer and closer, but never quite touches it. Truth is like the straight line forming the axis. A statement is like the curved line approaching it. The farther the curved line is from the straight line, the farther the statement is from the truth. The closer to the straight line, the closer to truth. The original author of this definition, Peirce, was, among other things, a geometer, so the analogy is probably intended.

What the author is expressing in a way so reminiscent of geometry becomes more lucid if interpreted as a way of explaining truth in terms of the traditional notion of induction. A universal statement is more nearly verified with each new supporting instance, but it is never completely verified. Although individual cases support a universal statement, that statement always involves a leap beyond the testimony they furnish.

The close relationship between the definition and induction suggests certain alterations in the wording of the definition which make clearer its meaning. It seems evident that "ideal limit" refers to perfect verification. It should, therefore, not distort the meaning to reword the definition as follows: "Truth is that concordance of an abstract statement with the ideal limit of perfect verification towards which endless investigation would tend to bring scientific belief . . ."

Now that a start has been made in making changes in the definition in the interests of greater clarity, are any other changes possible? The definition speaks of the concordance of an abstract statement with the ideal limit and then adds that endless investigation tends to bring scientific belief toward this limit. Both abstract statements and scientific beliefs are spoken of in the same way in respect to the limit. When an abstract statement agrees with the limit, we have truth. When a scientific belief tends toward that same limit, it tends toward truth. Furthermore, there is only one method of reaching the ideal limit, and that is the method of endless investigation. It seems plain, then, that the abstract statement and the scientific belief are really different sides of the same coin. Indeed, one gets this impression directly from simply reading the original definition. The abstract statement and the scientific belief are related such that the abstract statement is the statement *of* the belief. Since nothing in the definition turns on keeping clear the distinction of a belief from the statement of that belief, there should be no objection to using one term for both. "Truth is that concordance of an abstract statement with the ideal limit of perfect verification towards which endless investigation would tend to bring that statement . . ."

The passage still is awkward, and there are other changes which can be made to make it more intelligible. The "ideal limit of perfect verification" refers, of course, to the perfect verification of the abstract statement. We can, therefore, say, "Truth is that concordance of an abstract statement with the ideal limit of perfect verification of that statement towards which endless investigation would tend to bring that statement . . ."

The definition can be clarified further by deleting the unnecessary reference to a concordance. "Truth is the perfect verification of an abstract statement towards which endless investigation would tend to bring that statement . . ."

With the definition in this form certain defects appear. An obvious one, indeed, one that was apparent in the original form of the definition, is that the definition talks about truth only in reference to abstract statements. This means that a concrete statement such as, "The chains are in the trunk", is neither true nor false. However, unless there is some doubt whether what is in the trunk are chains or not, or if one does not have chains or a car with a trunk, there appears to be no way that such a statement could be neither true nor false.

Another defect is that the only method of verification allowed is that of induction. Perhaps this limitation is due to the fact that Dewey is thinking only of verifying abstract statements. This is not the place to try to settle the question regarding what kinds of verification there are. Limiting verification to induction, however, prevents deduction from performing that function and means, among other things, that most mathematical statements are not verifiable. In addition, one may wonder how the definition can allow for the common procedure of verifying a statement with only one or, at the most, a very few experiments.

The third and last defect is more serious than the others. The revised version of the definition begins, "Truth is the perfect verification . . ." Truth is identified with verification. Verification, however, is the testing of truth. It is understood that when one tests for something, regardless what it is, the test and that which is tested for are to be distinguished. To test for X implies that X is not identical with the testing for X. If X were identical with the testing for X, then, in order to test for X, one would have to test for the testing for X, and so on. To illustrate, let us suppose that we want to test a student's knowledge of botany. Clearly the knowledge we want to test and the test, itself, are two distinct things. A chemist may be interested in testing for dissolved minerals in the water supply. Obviously the minerals and his testing for them are distinct and different from each other. To confuse the two produces logical nonsense. The case is no different with truth and verification, regardless what kind of verification one has in mind. This confusion is an elementary mistake, but philosophers continue to make it with a persistence that is truly amazing.

Let us turn now to the last portion of the footnote which Dewey quotes from Peirce. For context, the part examined above is repeated. "Truth is that concordance of an abstract statement with the ideal limit towards which endless investigation would tend to bring scientific belief, which concordance the abstract statement may possess by virtue of the confession of its inaccuracy and one-sidedness, and this confession is an essential ingredient of truth." If one reads only the first half, the part we have been studying, it looks as if concordance admits of many degrees, but that it is never wholly present. However, the second part provides a way for a statement to have this concordance. This is quite a change to have occur, especially in the space of one sentence, and constitutes an inconsistency.

An abstract statement, it is said, has concordance by confessing that it is inaccurate and one-sided. The confession added to the abstract statement, however, is itself another statement so that we are dealing with not one, but two statements, and, in a sense, three. For example, let us say that the abstract statement is, "Water boils at 100° C." This statement as it stands is said not to have concordance with the ideal limit. It may, however, have this concordance by adding a confession of inaccuracy and one-sidedness.

C. { A. Water boils at 100° C.
         and
      B. this statement is inaccurate and one-sided.

Which of these statements is claimed to have concordance? The definition says, ". . . which concordance the abstract statement may possess by virtue of the confession of its inaccuracy and one-sidedness . . ." Is the confession a part of the statement which achieves concordance, or is it only the statement to which the confession is attached that achieves concordance? Perhaps a clue is furnished by the term, "abstract statement". In the first part of the definition "abstract statement" seems not to include the confession because the confession has not yet been introduced. In the second part we have the clear assertion that it is the abstract statement which possesses concordance. If the separate instances of the term, "abstract statement", refer to the same statement, as, of course, they should since they occur within the same sentence, then the statement which has concordance because of the confession is statement A, that is, "Water boils at 100° C."

There is, however, a strong objection to this interpretation. It seems that as a general principle, with one type of exception, we can say that the truth or falsity of a statement is not affected by another statement. The truth or falsity of the statement, "It is raining outside", is not affected by any other statement one might utter. Even statements such as, "I was only joking", or "Oh, I see the sprinkler was left on", do not change it. The type of exception referred to is made up of those statements which refer to another statement, as, for example, "No other statement follows this one." If another statement does follow, then the first statement is, of course, false. It is only in such cases that the truth of a statement can be affected by another statement. This exception, however, does not apply to our example, for sentence A refers to water and to when it boils. It does not refer to any statement. The truth of the statement, "Water boils at 100° C.", is, therefore, independent of the statement, "This statement is inaccurate and one-sided." This means that if, as the definition suggests, the sentence, "Water boils at 100° C.", does not have concordance and hence is not true, adding a confession will not make it true.

It would seem, therefore, that if any statement is true because of the confession, it must be the statement that includes the confession, that is, the statement about water boiling and the confession taken together, or statement C. Yet this cannot be so because the confession is directed toward A. That is, even if the confession could affect the truth of another statement, it would affect A because it is A that is confessed to be inaccurate. It is not the compound statement, C, that is confessed to be inaccurate. Whatever effect a confession of inaccuracy could have in producing truth, this effect is surely limited to that which is confessed to be inaccurate. Indeed, if it were to apply to C, then in addition to whatever else was confessed to be inaccurate, the confession confessed itself to be inaccurate. This would leave the reader totally puzzled as to what, in fact, was asserted since everything was said to be inaccurate.

As one reads the definition again, one is bothered by the suspicion that the trouble goes deeper than just an ambiguity about which statement has concordance. This more fundamental difficulty becomes clear if one uses the simple expedient of reducing the number of different terms used to refer to the same thing. The portion we are concerned about reads in the original version, ". . . which concordance the abstract statement may possess by virtue of the confession of its inaccuracy and one-sidedness . . ." To be inaccurate and one-sided, however, is simply to lack that concordance. Therefore, the passage may be restated as follows: ". . . which concordance the abstract statement may possess by virtue of the confession of its lack of concordance . . ." Since "truth" is defined in terms of concordance, this can again be reformulated: ". . . which truth the abstract statement may possess by virtue of the confession of its lack of truth . . ." Surely something is fundamentally wrong here. It certainly does not make sense to say that a sentence is true because it confesses that it is not true. The author has formulated a paradox, a logical impossibility.

Although there is little else to say concerning what is wrong with the definition, perhaps something might be offered concerning what may have prompted this definition. It seems likely that Dewey (and, of course, the original author, Peirce) wanted a definition of "truth" which would allow for the inaccuracy of statements of measurement and, more generally, one which would allow for constant reappraisal and revision in view of the rapid changes in the understanding of our world in recent times.

Let us look first at the former and take, by way of illustration, the statements, "Tom is six feet tall", and, "The voltage of this cell is 1.5 volts." One may very well wish to say, "Tom is six feet tall and this statement is inaccurate," because the yardstick is graduated only in sixteenths of an inch and a more finely graduated measure would likely have given a different reading.

One may make a similar statement about the voltage of a cell because, although a voltmeter registers 1.5 volts, a millivoltmeter would almost certainly have shown a different reading. Indeed, any actual measurement of a continuum in terms of discrete units may be suspected of inaccuracy because it is always possible that smaller units would give a different reading. Added to this kind of inaccuracy is the inaccuracy due to the measuring instrument's distorting the thing measured (as when a voltmeter decreases voltage because some of the current passes through it) and the inaccuracy of measuring things which are always changing (as measuring the level of a fluid in a vessel when the fluid is constantly evaporating). There are, of course, other kinds of inaccuracies as well. Since we have, with the rise of science, become more conscious of our inaccuracies, it is at least plausible that one would like to allow for them by admitting in the statement of measurement that it is inaccurate. Inaccuracy in measurement and inaccuracy in a statement of that measurement are, however, two quite different things. While inaccuracy in measurement may be unavoidable, inaccuracy in statements of measurement can be avoided. The error in the definition we are studying is that it advocates the wrong method. It has already been pointed out that a confession of inaccuracy does not make the original statement true. However, the statement of measurement can be formulated so that it does not claim more precision than the measurement has, for example, "Tom is six feet tall, plus or minus one-sixteenth of an inch", or, more simply, "Tom is approximately six feet tall." These statements are not inaccurate, and they do not lead to any paradox.

The other kind of statement mentioned above is that kind in which one hedges a conclusion because he thinks it likely later investigation will make it incorrect. Statements of measurement belong within this classification, of course, but also such statements as, "The cause of the common cold is the virus X", or, "Weather can be predicted far in advance by the study of solar flares." Here again, to safeguard against error one might be tempted to attach a confession of inaccuracy and one-sidedness. Unfortunately, however, this does not really prevent error.

A final criticism pertains to the entire footnote which Dewey borrows from Peirce and is implicit in the very organization of this chapter. This footnote contains three quite different definitions of "truth". Since what is true is different under each definition, they are inconsistent, one with another.

B. TRUTH AS DETERMINED BY CONSEQUENCES[3]

The popular understanding of Dewey's pragmatic theory of truth is that an idea is true if it works and that truth is determined by consequences. Dewey certainly did hold these views, but on different occasions he made other claims about truth as well. These other claims restrict the domain of truth by restricting the kinds of consequences which establish truth. There are four such claims or restrictions. Consequences which establish the truth of an idea must be the ones which the idea intends; they must be the ones that the idea claims; they must be operationally instituted; and they must solve the problem.

It is difficult to ascertain from Dewey's writings whether he regarded each restriction as being itself sufficient to establish truth or whether he meant that the four must be taken collectively to perform that function. Accordingly, we shall consider them individually and collectively.

Our first group of quotations merely asserts the importance of consequences in matter concerning truth.

According to experimental inquiry, the validity of the object of thought depends upon the *consequences* of the operations which define the object of thought.[4]

Confirmation, corroboration, verification lie in works, consequences. Handsome is that handsome does. By their fruits shall ye *know* them.[5]

---

[3] A similar version, but with the title, "Dewey's Theory of Truth", appeared in the Spring, 1965 issue of *The Personalist*.
[4] John Dewey, *The Quest for Certainty: A Study of the Relation of Knowledge and Action*, Capricorn edition (New York, 1960), pp. 128-129.
[5] John Dewey, *Reconstruction in Philosophy*, Beacon edition (Boston, 1957), p. 156.

... the pragmatic contention that these consequences define the meaning of truth . . .[6]

But I again affirm that the term "pragmatic" means only the rule of referring all thinking, all reflective considerations, to *consequences* for final meaning and test. Nothing is said about the nature of the consequences; they may be aesthetic, or moral, or political, or religious in quality – anything you please. All that the theory requires is that they be in some way consequences of thinking; not, indeed, of it alone, but of it acted upon in connection with other things.[7]

Each of these passages assigns to consequences the function of establishing whether or not "the object of thought", "thinking", or "reflective consideration" is true. Of course, to say that consequences test ideas is not to say how they will distinguish the true from the false.

An advance is made when Dewey adds, "The hypothesis that works in the *true* one . . ." [8] This statement differentiates the right kind of consequences from the wrong kind. The expression, "pragmatic", which Dewey chose to characterize his theory of truth, also suggests a theory in terms of what works or is useful. On one occasion he defines "truth" in much this way, saying, ". . . when truth is defined as utility . . ." [9]

This preliminary formulation of the pragmatic theory of truth has been the principal target for critics – and it has been an easy target, for it is obvious that an idea may be useful even though it is not true. However, although Dewey says that a true idea is useful, he does not mean that any idea which is useful is true, for he says, "The usefulness of a road is not measured by the degree in which it lends itself to the purposes of a highwayman . . . And so with the serviceableness of an idea or hypothesis as a measure of its truth." [10] Only certain uses are relevant. The conventional criticism of the pragmatic theory of truth, therefore, misses the mark, for it censures a position which Dewey does not hold. The

[6] John Dewey, *Essays in Experimental Logic*, Dover edition (New York), p. 318.
[7] Dewey, *Essays*, p. 330.
[8] Dewey, *Reconstruction*, p. 156.
[9] Dewey, *Reconstruction*, p. 157.
[10] Dewey, *Reconstruction*, pp. 157-158.

several restrictions which Dewey places on consequences, restrictions which are the concern of the rest of this chapter, should be regarded as an enrichment of his concept of what it is for an idea to work.

The first of Dewey's four restrictions on consequences is that they must be intended by the idea. In the following passage consequences which establish truth are limited ostensibly to those that satisfy and are good, but actually, to what the ideas intend: ". . . I have never identified any satisfaction with the truth of an idea, save *that* satisfaction which arises when the idea as working hypothesis or tentative method is applied to prior existences in such a way as to fulfill what it intends." [11] The burden of this passage surely lies in saying that the idea ". . . is applied to prior existences in such a way as to fulfill what it intends." Translated in terms of consequences, this says that only those consequences which the idea intends to produce are relevant to the establishment of truth. Although Dewey began the passage as if verification were to be explained in terms of satisfaction, in describing the kind of satisfaction he wants, he makes it clear (although this may not be intentional) that satisfaction is quite unnecessary. If, for example, someone reported that he felt no satisfaction at all even though his inquiry terminated in the very consequence he intended when formulating his hypothesis, Dewey would surely not regard that hypothesis as unverified. Satisfaction is presented as an unessential by-product of finding just those consequences which the idea intends.

In another passage Dewey appears to tie the correct consequences to goodness, just as in the foregoing he appeared to tie them to satisfaction. The real tie, however, is between a consequence and what an idea intends and claims; for the goodness turns out to be such a special kind that it, like satisfaction, is irrelevant. In the midst of discussing William James' book, *Pragmatism, A New Name for Some Old Ways of Thinking*, Dewey writes,

Difficulties have arisen chiefly because Mr. James is charged with . . . arguing that since true ideas are good, any idea if good in any way is

[11] Dewey, *Essays*, p. 320

true. Certainly transition from one of these conceptions to the other is facilitated by the fact that ideas are tested as to their validity by a certain goodness, viz., whether they are good for accomplishing what they intend, for what they claim to be good for, that is, certain modifications in prior given existences.[12]

A page later this point is made again: "If an idea leads to consequences which are good in the *one* respect only of fulfilling the intent of the idea (as when one drinks a liquid to test the idea that it is a poison), does the badness of the consequences in every other respect detract from the verifying force of consequences?"[13] Dewey expects, of course, a negative reply. The consequences being good are, for Dewey, nothing more than that the consequences are what the idea intends them to be. Clearly, it is as unimportant to call these consequences "good" as it is to call them "satisfying".

Another statement does with the term, "utility", what the foregoing ones have done with "goodness" and "satisfying". It is also the most concise of the three. "As matter of fact, truth as utility means service in making just that contribution to reorganization in experience that the idea or theory claims to be able to make."[14] The expression, "contributions to reorganization in experience", presumably means the same as the more common one, "consequences".

In these passages Dewey does not seem to draw a distinction between what an idea intends and what an idea claims. "Intends" and "claims" seem to be used as synonyms. Against the possibility, however, that they are not intended as synonyms, they shall be examined separately, with different interpretations for each.

That which an idea intends presumably is what the inquirer who has the idea intends. The restriction that intention places on the tie between consequences and truth, then, is that only those consequences are relevant to truth which are what the inquirer intends. If, when the idea is acted upon, a consequence occurs which the inquirer does not intend, this consequence neither establishes nor disestablishes the truth of that idea.

---

[12] Dewey, *Essays*, pp. 318-319.
[13] Dewey, *Essays*, p. 320.
[14] Dewey, *Reconstruction*, p. 157.

With this restriction placed on the consequences, is it possible to find an exception? Is it possible to find an idea which is plainly false even though acting on it produces the intended consequences? Exceptions are numerous, but one will suffice. A man, let us say, is ill with tuberculosis. His physician believes him to have pneumonia. Intending to make him well, the physician administers penicillin, and in due time the patient becomes well. Because the intended consequence occurred, the idea that the patient had pneumonia must have been true. Nevertheless, he had not pneumonia, but tuberculosis.

In the passages quoted earlier it was observed that Dewey also restricted consequences which establish truth to those claimed by the idea. If one understands this to mean that only those consequences are relevant which the inquirer, if asked, would claim would occur, then there is no real difference between what an idea claims and what it intends. There are, however, other ways of understanding the expression, "what an idea claims".

Because Dewey contends elsewhere that all ideas must be symbolized,[15] we can learn what ideas claim by referring to the usual mode of symbolization, our common language, and asking the question, "What do statements claim?" What does the statement, "It is raining", claim? A plausible reply is that the statement claims that it is raining. It claims what it explicitly says – which is why its claim can be expressed by repeating the statement in the form of a clause beginning with "that". One knows what a statement claims when he understands the statement. A statement claims what it says, and an idea claims what the statement which expresses it says.

The next question is, "What consequences do ideas claim?" This question presupposes something that is not the case. It presupposes that all ideas claim consequences. As a matter of fact, only those ideas which talk about consequences can be said to claim consequences. In the context of inquiry, which is, of course, the only context Dewey allows for ideas, this limits the ideas which claim consequences to those which state that if something is done, something else will result. Let us suppose that the problem

[15]   Dewey, *Logic*, p. 110.

at hand is to learn the nature of electricity. A proposed solution, which is, therefore, an idea, is "Electricity is a fluid." Since this statement does not mention any consequences, it claims none. Another idea might be, "If electricity of constant voltage is passed through wires of different diameters, an ammeter will show that less current passes through the smaller wire than the larger one." This idea does claim a consequence. Dewey has said that only those consequences verify an idea which the idea claims as consequences. Examination shows, however, that only the second of the two kinds of ideas actually claims any consequences at all. The first kind, proposed solutions which do not claim consequences, are, then, without a means of verification.

In respect to those ideas which do claim consequences, a further distinction must be drawn. The kind of idea in mind says that if one does X, Y will result. If, in order for Y to be the consequence of doing X, it is necessary that the person actually do X, i.e., correctly act on the idea, then there are no exceptions to this version of the theory. Suppose that the problem is that one's auto is mired. The solution proposed is that if one puts on chains he will get out. If one acts correctly on the idea, i.e., if he puts on the chains, and if the consequence occurs, i.e., if he gets out, then the idea is true. There is no doubt but that this method of verification is sound. The interesting thing is that this test is precisely the one that defines "truth" for one of Dewey's several antagonists, the advocate of the correspondence theory of truth. On the one hand, there is the idea that if one puts on chains, he will get out; and on the other hand, there are the occurrences of putting on chains and getting out. This version of the theory seems to be a distinctively pragmatic method of verification because it refers to consequences, but the peculiar ideas, actions, and consequences which are required to illustrate this method also illustrate the correspondence theory of truth.

On the other hand, if Y can be a consequence of doing X even though X is not actually done, i.e., the idea is not acted upon correctly, then there are numerous exceptions to this version of the pragmatic theory. Suppose that the problem is whether water is inflammable. The idea is that if one drops a lighted match into

a can of water, there will be a fire. The can, however, is unmark-
ed, and the experimenter unwittingly drops the lighted match into
a can of gasoline. The consequence is that there is a fire. According to that version of the theory under consideration, the idea
that water is inflammable is true because the claimed consequence actually occurred. Nevertheless, the idea is patently false.

We have interpreted the expression, "what an idea claims", as
being what the statement of that idea explicitly claims. Perhaps
a more liberal reading is more appropriate. Perhaps Dewey means
that those consequences are relevant to truth which the idea, in
a broad sense, implies. Therefore, although the idea that a sick
child has measles does not explicitly mention consequences, it can
be said to claim a consequence because it implies that the child
has a fever. It is clear, however, that a fever could accompany
other diseases as well as measles. The implied consequence may
occur even though the child has not measles, but pneumonia. The
failure of implied consequences to determine truth becomes even
more apparent when we consider how many things ideas imply.
The idea that the child has measles also implies that he will not
attend school the next day. He may, in fact, not attend the next
day for any number of reasons so that his absence is of little
value in determining whether or not he is now sick because of
measles.

A further development of what it means for an idea to work is
found in the qualification that consequences which establish an
idea as true must be operationally instituted.

> Then arises the theory that ideas as ideas are always working hy-
> potheses concerning the attaining of particular empirical results, and
> are tentative programs (or sketches of method) for attaining them. If
> we stick consistently to this notion of ideas, only *consequences which
> are actually produced by the working of the idea in co-operation with,
> or application to, prior existences are good consequences in the
> specific sense of good which is relevant to establishing the truth of an
> idea.*[16]

> But in the proper interpretation of "pragmatic", namely the function
> of consequences as necessary tests of the validity of propositions,

[16] Dewey, *Essays*, p. 319.

provided these consequences are operationally instituted and are such as to resolve the specific problem evoking the operations, the text that follows is thoroughly pragmatic.[17]

The second passage makes two points, one of which is that the consequences must be such that they "resolve the specific problem evoking the operations". This matter will be taken up shortly. The other point, a point which the first passage delineates more clearly, is that the consequences which test the truth of an idea must be "operationally instituted". This restriction was no doubt added in order to exclude accidental consequences.

Presumably consequences may be accidental or not operationally instituted in one of two overlapping ways: they might not be caused by the operation, or they might not be intended by the inquirer. The deficiency of a theory of truth based on the latter has been already demonstrated. It remains only to ask whether a theory of truth can be based on the former, i.e., whether an idea is unfailingly true if acting upon it is the cause of the consequences.

Apparently any action has some consequence or other. So long as the action is an "acting on the idea" (Dewey's somewhat vague, but only, stipulation regarding which actions are allowed), then any idea is true, for one can always find some consequence which is, in fact, caused by acting on that idea. Consider the idea that a man can fly by flapping his arms. This idea, let us say, leads to the action of jumping from a high ledge, and this action, in turn, is the cause of breaking a leg. Therefore, according to this particular version of the pragmatic theory of truth, the idea that a man can fly by flapping his arms is true because the consequence (breaking the leg) was operationally instituted (was caused) by acting on that idea (jumping from the ledge). Quite obviously this version of the theory needs mending.

A final group of passages pertains to that version of the pragmatic theory of truth which states that the consequences which verify an idea are those which solve the problem. In the passage quoted above this theme was introduced. In the following one it is stated emphatically:

[17] Dewey, *Logic*, p. iv.

If ideas, meanings, conceptions, notions, theories, systems are instrumental to an active reorganization of the given environment, to a removal of some specific trouble and perplexity, then the test of their validity and value lies in accomplishing this work. If they succeed in their office, they are reliable, sound, valid, good, true. If they fail to clear up confusion, to eliminate defects, if they increase confusion, uncertainty and evil when they are acted upon, then are they false.[18]

On another occasion Dewey writes that consequences test the validity of an idea only when they ". . . are such as to resolve the specific problem evoking the operations . . ." [19]

Are there any exceptions to this last version of the pragmatic theory of truth? If this version is made to stand alone, as were the other three, exceptions are not hard to find. Suppose that a person is ill with twenty-four hour influenza. The problem is to regain health. The patient prescribes for himself a dose of honey and vinegar in the belief that this concoction will effect a cure. A day later, the disease having run its natural course, he is, indeed, well. The consequence (becoming well) solved the problem; nevertheless, the idea that honey and vinegar would work a cure was not true. Incidentally, this example points to the need for the restriction requiring that the consequence be operationally instituted.

Dewey's theory of truth is considerably more acceptable if the several restrictions concerning the consequences which verify an idea are taken conjunctively instead of individually. Are there any cases in which an idea is clearly not true even though (1) the consequence of acting on that idea is intended, (2) the consequence is claimed, (3) the consequence is operationally instituted, and (4) the consequence solves the problem? Suppose that a hiker is lost and only one path leads to his destination. The problem is to arrive at his destination. His idea, let us say, is that by taking the fourth path on the right he will reach his destination. In acting on this idea he takes the third path by mistake, but, nevertheless, arrives at his destination. The consequence (arriving at his destination) was the one intended and claimed.

18 Dewey, *Reconstruction*, p. 156.
19 Dewey, *Logic*, p. iv.

It was also operationally instituted (was caused by acting on the idea), and it certainly solved the problem. According to the theory, the idea that by taking the fourth path on the right he will reach his destination was true. Nevertheless, it was really the third path which led to his destination.

Dewey allows the concept of acting on an idea to be sufficiently imprecise so that it seems that one may choose incorrectly in what he does and yet be said to be acting on that idea. The above example, which seems to be a legitimate exception to this, the most acceptable form of the pragmatic theory of truth, depends on such imprecision in order to be an exception. This prompts one to ask, "Would not the pragmatic theory of truth be impregnable if the concept of acting on an idea were changed so that mistakes were ruled out?" Besides the suspicion that it either would involve inquiry in an infinite series of inquiries or would implicitly rely on the correspondence theory of truth, this revised theory is subject to disproving examples. Suppose that a certain book is lost. The problem is finding it. The idea, let us say, is that the book is on the bottom shelf. In acting on this idea, i.e., looking on the bottom shelf, the book is found behind the shelf on the floor. The consequence (finding the book) was intended, it was claimed (in the sense of being implied), it was operationally instituted, and it solved the problem. Furthermore, the manner in which the person acted upon the idea (looking for the book on the bottom shelf) involved no error. According to the theory, then, the idea that the book is on the bottom shelf should have been true; yet the book was not on the bottom shelf, but on the floor.

A theory of truth which is not merely a re-definition of "true" must meet two minimal conditions. First, there must be no cases which are obviously true, but which do not meet the demands of the theory. Secondly, there must be no cases which meet the demands of the theory, but which are obviously not true. The exceptions offered to the various versions of Dewey's pragmatic theory of truth show that none of these versions meets the second condition except for one which supports equally well the correspondence theory of truth.

INDEX

74950